Body
Building

BOOKS IN THE LEADERSHIP INSIGHT SERIES

Body Building: Creating a Ministry Team Through Spiritual Gifts
Brian Kelley Bauknight

The Pastor's Start-Up Manual: Beginning a New Pastorate
Robert H. Ramey, Jr.

LEADERSHIP *LIS* INSIGHT SERIES
LEADERSHIP *LIS* INSIGHT SERIES
LEADERSHIP *LIS* INSIGHT SERIES

Body Building

Creating a Ministry Team
Through Spiritual Gifts

HERB MILLER, EDITOR

A moment of insight is worth a lifetime of experience

LINCOLN CHRISTIAN·COLLEGE **AND SEMINARY**

BRIAN KELLEY BAUKNIGHT

Abingdon Press
Nashville

BODY BUILDING

Copyright © 1996 by Abingdon Press

This book is printed on recycled, acid-free paper.

Library of Congress Cataloging-in-Publication Data
Bauknight, Brian Kelley, 1939–
    Body building: creating a ministry team through spiritual gifts/
Brian Kelley Bauknight: Herb Miller, editor.
      p. cm.—(Leadership insights series)
    Includes bibliographical references.
    ISBN 0-687-01710-6 (pbk.: alk. paper)
    1. Group ministry.   2. Gifts, Spiritual.   3. Christian leadership.
4. Lay ministry.   5. Bible. O.T. Ephesians   IV. 11-12—Criticism,
interpretation, etc.   I. Miller, Herb.   II. Title.   III. Series.
BV675.B38   1996
253—dc20

95-31956
CIP

Scripture quotations, unless otherwise indicated, are from the New Revised Standard Version Bible, copyright © 1989, by the Division of Christian Education of the National Council of the Churches of Christ in the United States of America. Used by permission.

Scripture quotations noted GNB are from the *Good News Bible*—Old Testament: Copyright © American Bible Society 1976; New Testament: Copyright © American Bible Society 1966, 1971, 1976. Used by permission.

Scripture quotations noted RSV are from the Revised Standard Version of the Bible, copyright 1946, 1952, 1971 by the Division of Christian Education of the National Council of Churches of Christ in the USA. Used by permission.

96 97 98 99 00 01 02 03 04 05 — 10 9 8 7 6 5 4 3 2 1

MANUFACTURED IN THE UNITED STATES OF AMERICA

With gratitude to all
who have cared for me, encouraged me, and
remained steadfast in ministry with me at
Christ United Methodist Church
Bethel Park, Pennsylvania

CONTENTS

FOREWORD

Realizing that he was on the wrong road, a traveler in northern Vermont stopped in a village and said to a passerby, "I need your help. I'm lost."

The villager asked, "Do you know where you are?"

"Yes," said the traveler. "I saw the name of your village when I drove into town."

"Do you know where you want to go?" the pedestrian asked.

"Yes," the traveler replied, naming his destination.

"You ain't lost," the villager responded philosophically. "You just need directions."

Most church leaders recognize the importance of networking with the ministry giftedness of members and staff. Like the Vermont traveler, they are not lost. They just need directions. Bauknight unfolds a map and highlights the roads that lead to effectiveness in this leadership role. Grounded in biblical theology, his ideas speak to congregations of all sizes. His concepts are especially helpful to pastors in multiple-staff congregations, most of whose educational preparations provided them no charts of this territory.

God gave Moses the vision to build the tabernacle, but Moses did not do that by himself. God gave him Bezalel, who had "skill, intelligence, and knowledge in every kind of craft" (Exod. 35:31). God gave Ezra the vision to lead Israel in rebuilding their society after the Babylonian captivity, but

Ezra did not do that by himself. "I gathered leaders from Israel to go up with me" (Ezra 7:28). Jesus used the same procedure to change the world. He put together a twelve-person team.

Many Americans who visit Washington, D.C. marvel at Gutzon Borglum's huge head of Lincoln. While Borglum was sculpting Lincoln's face from a massive piece of stone, a family visited his studio. The five-year-old daughter, gazing in wonder at the granite block, tugged at Borglum's pants leg. "Is that Abraham Lincoln?" she asked.

"Yes," he replied.

"How did you know he was in there?" she asked.

Church leaders engage in a similar endeavor. They must (a) see what is inside other potential leaders, (b) use leadership skill to bring it out, and (c) avoid standing in front of it, once that skill becomes obvious to others.

Bauknight gives us directions for strengthening that ability.

—Herb Miller, Lubbock, Texas

ACKNOWLEDGMENTS

Other writers and leaders have touched upon the recommendations presented in these pages. I am especially grateful to the late Quaker writer, Robert Greenleaf, for his basic book *Servant Leadership: A Journey into the Nature of Legitimate Power and Greatness.*

I also acknowledge with appreciation three distinguished teachers who have prompted and prodded me along the way: Lyle Schaller, Ronald Sunderland, and Herb Miller. I owe a debt of gratitude to Marjorie Suhocki, who directed the Doctor of Ministry Program at Pittsburgh Theological Seminary some years ago. She persuasively insisted that everything we do in ministry must be subjected to critical theological reflection.

The steadfast friendship of Leah Bergstrom, whose pilgrimage is documented in these pages, has been a source of joy and confidence in my ministry. I am thankful for Cindy Olszewski, a key lay staff associate on my current leadership team. She pushed me toward clarity and consistency in the early years of my stumbling efforts toward leadership at Christ Church. Our working relationship is built upon honesty, risk taking, and mutual trust.

I am thankful to a cluster of corporate executives who welcomed and challenged me upon my arrival in Bethel Park in 1980. They gave me the freedom to be the kind of leader God seemed to be building within my spirit.

Acknowledgments

An informal annual "gathering" of senior ministers of larger membership churches in my denomination deserves special recognition. They gave me spiritual and emotional sustenance at the beginning of my present ministry. These colleagues are a rich resource for critical examination of my commitments to a particular kind of leadership. Our time together each fall is invaluable. I have a greater confidence in God's grace and guiding hand because of them.

Finally, I thank God for my wife, Elaine, who has gently prodded me toward the writing of this book. She may have believed in the value of this offering even more than I. Her love encouraged and sustained me through the difficult and cumbersome hours of gathering thoughts, writing, editing, critiquing, and rewriting. She knew I could write this book because I was living it in my day-to-day ministry.

INTRODUCTION

EVERY LEADER A SERVANT

person'

The theological assumptions and administrative style outlined in this book have been evolving over more than twenty years. However, the principal foundation remains unchanged: *Every clergy leader is the servant of God's gifts to God's people. This understanding of ministry both builds and renews the Body of Christ.*

The resulting principles have guided me to a practical theology of church organization and a fresh way of doing ministry. Grounded in the sacred writings of the earliest church, this "theology of church formation" builds on present trends in church leadership development while propelling us toward change in the twenty-first century.

For the first ten years of my ministry, I labored with as much diligence as God made possible in arenas where God seemed to call. The local church demanded proficiency as preacher, pastor, priest, administrator, fund-raiser, Sunday school overseer, Bible teacher, and denominational advocate. I was a generalist, and that experience brought fulfillment.

Early in my second decade of ministry, I began connecting with a fresh leadership style. As the Spirit nudged me, I discovered a form for ministry which (a) seems to be faithful to the plan and purpose of God, and (b) can be utilized in congregations of every size and configuration. The resultant leadership concept now guides almost every aspect of my local church ministry.

My Trip to the Concept

Biblical leadership designations such as "pastor," "shepherd," "presbyter," and "apostle" seem disconnected from our contemporary setting. More modern descriptive titles for clergy such as "minister," "enabler," or "facilitator" seem similarly inadequate for this generation. We now search for new labels by which to describe the work of the ordained clergy. None of the previous designations have demonstrated durability or captured long-term imagination.

Likewise, secular designations such as "manager," "chief executive officer," "chief operating officer," or "corporate head" leave a cold and colorless imprint upon the work of the Christian church. I observe growing discomfort with organizational charts and hierarchical modes of understanding ministry.

Several prototypes of secular leadership models were gently thrust upon me by committed men and women in the early days of my present church appointment. Reasons for growing discomfort with their suggestions were not easy to discern. In fact, I initially accepted as normative the styles and methods they proposed. After all, many of them were highly successful captains of industry, and I had much to learn. However, their proposed methods and models wore thin within about two years. Many procedures that sound so good in secular theory become counterproductive when practiced in church settings.

The Collegial Pyramid

Surely, a methodology of leadership exists that matches God's unique creation of the church and is discernible in Scripture. This book presents one such leadership style. In its most simplistic organizational description, the style is collegial, but with a pyramidic overlay.

The leadership model documented here recognizes God's creative gifts for each individual—for the laity and the employed leadership team alike. The pattern also acknowledges the need for an overseer, someone who carries comprehensive responsibility for the total ministry. The overseer, however, does not dominate his or her colleagues. Subordination is not appropriate. Rather, all are gifted by God to form the congregation's ministry. The designated leader is simply "first among equals."

Primarily, the style advocated on these pages calls forth and utilizes the spiritual gifts of God's people. In the most authentic meaning of the term, the church leadership style presented here is "charismatic." Such a paradigm is always fluid, but appropriate to the church that is faithful to the call of God.

CHAPTER 1

GROUNDINGS

At the close of a weekday Bible study, I spoke with Leah regarding the church's much-discussed need for some level of "educational assistant." She had recently stepped down from full-time teaching in the public schools in order to begin a family. She and her husband demonstrated a mature understanding of stewardship of time, talent, and resources. They seemed ready for some call to a larger ministry. Her response to my conversation that day was instantaneous. "I cannot tell you why," she said, "but I believe that God is calling me to some kind of vocation in the church right now. I'd like to give that job a try."

The church had little to offer her by way of financial compensation. Even less was available in terms of office space in which to work. The congregation was small (about two hundred members) and only recently released from outside mission support. For the first time, the congregation was fully responsible for the total costs of ministry.

Neither the personnel committee nor I had any experience in staffing a church. However, after considerable discussion through the labyrinth of proper church channels, Leah began work as an educational assistant. She quickly became an essential part of the growing ministry of that congregation.

In the two-plus decades since that day, Leah blossomed vigorously under God's grace. That congregation now has one of the largest United Methodist Sunday schools in Pennsylvania—including large numbers of adult classes. Long after this pastor's tenure at the church, she is a highly effective pastoral presence in the congregation, exercising multiple gifts. First consecrated as a diaconal minister, she recently completed seminary training and is now ordained. Her gifts for the work of ministry continue to expand according to God's gracious intent.

This story paints a living picture of the three presuppositions on which this book stands. *First, the church is a creation of God, a masterpiece of God's design.* I make no claims to special insight regarding a blueprint for the church within the mind of God. However, the biblical witness seems clear: Jesus called a band of followers out of the world, trained them in fundamental elements of discipleship, and sent them back into the world as agents of change. Through the local church, his mission continues into our day.

Jesus taught the earliest disciples to lean into the Holy Spirit. He taught them the good news of saving grace. He encouraged them to nurture their communion with God. He called them to ministries of justice and compassion. Jesus instructed them to facilitate ministries of inward growth as well as outward service. The contemporary church continues to bear a primary task within these same parameters.

We who are called to discipleship in this moment of history can only hope to build a model that reflects the original design for the church in the will of God. To do that, we must study and meditate upon the great texts. We must work to discover the power and promise of the gathered congregation of believers in this age. With care, sensitivity, and reverent imagination we must try to relate the first century interpretation of God's activity to the closing years of the twentieth century and beyond.

A second presupposition is this: *Ephesians is a "manual" for bringing the church into being and for growing a body of believers.* This New Testament writing is a first century communication about the matter of being the church. Rather than speaking to a particular local situation, Ephesians is directed *to* the church as a whole. Probably not written solely to one congregation, the letter seems to have been circulated to all congregations over time.[1] The letter may have been the first century equivalent of *The Book of Discipline* (United Methodist) or *Book of Order* (Presbyterian USA), but without the need for meticulous and voluminous detail.

The third presupposition: *Ephesians 4:11-12 is a declaration regarding the direction in which the church should be moving.* "The gifts [God] gave were that some would be apostles, some prophets, some evangelists, some pastors and teachers, to equip the saints for the work of ministry, for building up the body of Christ." These ancient words define objectives for every pastor and Christian leader. They clarify our insight into the term "charismatic," and point to untapped resources. God gives gifts in abundance to every believer. Church leadership is mostly a matter of letting spiritual gifts do their ministry.

Beginning Insights

The implications of the Ephesians text began to grow during the early stages of my second pastorate, almost ten years beyond my ordination.[2] My physical energies and skills would simply not meet the ever-expanding needs for ministry in the community. The congregation contained many young households. Their abounding energy and high levels of commitment to the church flourished in the midst of suburban lifestyles. Whoever led that congregation would quickly fragment or experience early burnout—unless he or she could find alternatives to the traditional pastoral roles. The diverse requirements for preaching, church school, program development, new member assimilation, leadership training, fellowship, finances, long-range capital development and outreach left little time to develop pastoral strengths.

While continuing to be enthusiastic about the opportunities for ministry in that church, I wondered if anyone could really cultivate and harness the potential among those people. For that matter, could it be done in *any* active or growing congregation?

One seed for the answer to that question was planted in my conversation with Leah recalled at the beginning of this chapter. Hers was not an isolated story. In the ensuing years, the same scenario multiplied many times through that congregation. Eight part-time laypersons were called into specific ministries over the next seven years—as needs arose in areas of music, youth, membership cultivation and care, volunteer coordination, and financial oversight. Persons in widely varied stages of life exhibited gifts: a retired accountant, an empty nester, an elementary school teacher with a love for music, a young mother, and a recently graduated civil engineer.

Of crucial note: *each individual who came into the leadership team of that congregation had formal membership ties with that church.* Each one elected to exercise spiritual gifts in a very specific way as a call of God. Some were initially volunteers, and some remained so. Others were modestly compensated for their work from the beginning. One received a small stipend and then returned it to the church.

These gifted persons called other members of the congregation to arenas of service and ministry. A host of lay leaders and workers emerged as more gifts were identified, called forth, and trained. The gifts of the Spirit multiplied. Measurable results spread from within the system.

When I arrived in a third setting, I was determined to use this same theology of administration. The spiritual gifts of the laity demanded full attention. However, I had no assurance that what had happened at my former church could be transferred into a new situation. My methodology was especially problematic in a congregation nearly four times bigger. Furthermore, morale was sagging due to multiple clergy transitions during recent years.

In the first years of that new pastorate, I studied the design of the primitive church. I researched biblical texts and literature concerning spiritual gifts in that context. I examined Jesus' servant-leader style, and the strengths of its application in the infant church. Persistent questions from the previous years of ministry reappeared. Did the practice of leadership I had discovered apply universally? Or, was it only applicable to the peculiarities of one congregation? Were the answers unique to a growing congregation in suburbia? Could these principles nurture any congregation in any time and place? Could results be forthcoming where no deliberate precedent for this form of ministry had yet taken shape?

I am persuaded that leadership through spiritual gifts is applicable and appropriate in every congregation.

Christ United Methodist Church of Bethel Park, Pennsylvania, is a congregation of about three thousand members ten miles south of downtown Pittsburgh. The church has not experienced rapid numerical growth, although membership has increased by a net of about four hundred persons in the past eight years. The *exciting* growth has been in expanded ministry and mission—the fruit of called, trained, and implemented spiritual gifts.

Fifteen years ago, five clergy, one diaconal musician, and three part-time lay professionals *directed* the ministry of the church. Today, three clergy and nine full-time or nearly full-time lay program staff *oversee* the ministry of the church.[3] Most important, each staff member recruits, trains, and provides moments of appreciation for the spiritual gifts among scores of laity who serve in innumerable ways.

Sixty lay pastors (see chapter 3) provide care for temporary and extended pastoral needs under clergy assignment and support. More than two hundred children, youth, and adults express their gifts through the music of the choirs—and are regularly acknowledged in this capacity. Volunteer workers with youth are recruited and utilized because they have gifts for (a) ongoing programming and youth ministry or (b) gifts for special events such as work camps, retreat weekends, or service projects. Multiple office volunteers are called and trained by a volunteer coordinator—herself having the gifts of encouragement and organization for this significant task.

New dimensions of ministry may *begin* with staff initiative and hands-on direction. However, members with specific gifts are soon pursued for special oversight. Examples include a covenant group ministry, adult education, an alternative gift mart, hunger related projects, vacation Bible school, and support group facilitation. Each new level of ministry or mission necessitates a renewed search for the right spiritual gifts for lay leadership.

Extension ministries of the church emerge in similar fashion. A five component weekday child care ministry thrives based on spiritual gifts of administrative leadership and many volunteers. A two-phase adult day care and Alzheimer's unit emerged from the visionary gifts of one woman. That ministry now serves the needs of the frail elderly and their families because of the spiritual gifts of those who care about persons on the margins of life. A single adult ministry began because of the energy and vision of one clergywoman. Today, that ministry thrives under clergy direction *and* a strong single adult council. Leadership gifts for this ministry are constantly in training.

Ephesians 4:11-12 forms the biblical and theological framework for a working ecclesiology in ministry throughout the church. The foundation is appropriately and necessarily centered in the person and work of Jesus Christ. "We must grow up in every way *into him who is the head, into Christ*" (Eph. 4:15, *emphasis mine*).

Prayer and preaching are essential building blocks. Prayer disciplines are of crucial importance. Without prayer, the foundation crumbles. Preaching must regularly address the issue of spiritual gifts. People who recognize and practice an ecclesiology of spiritual gifts find encouragement and hope. Calling forth a person's spiritual gifts results in a thriving, satisfying, and fruitful Christian life.

The Paid Volunteer

Beverly is a wife and the mother of three grown daughters. She finds comfort and devotional meaning in daily segments of time at the piano keyboard. She plays an extensive repertoire of popular secular and sacred music, moving easily from piece to piece without needing sheet music. Her style of playing provides pleasant listening.

When we began a Saturday evening alternative worship service, we asked Beverly to provide piano music for this service. Worshipers responded enthusiastically. She quickly became an integral part of a significant worship menu for the congregation.

Beverly began coming twenty minutes early each Saturday evening to play for those who arrived early. Dozens of persons intentionally use this opportunity for meditation and preparation for worship.

Soon, a folk choir was added to that service. In addition to singing voices, the folk choir includes guitars, banjo, bass, recorder, and two harmonica players. Each week a new combination of instruments delights the congregation.

Beverly now receives a small stipend for her musical offering at the keyboard. In response, she provides service information (themes, texts, etc.) to the folk choir, recruits special music when the choir is not available, recruits her vacation replacements, and provides some logistical oversight to the service. She rejoices in the use of her gifts.

Letting the Light Shine

A Sunday school teacher asked the children if they knew what a "saint" was. After a short pause, one child said, "A saint is someone who lets the light shine through." Saints comprise the membership of every congregation. When those saints let the light of God's gifts shine through, marvelous and unexpected things happen.

Some church leaders fret that a growing church is one that accommodates itself culturally. In the attempt to attract the unchurched, they worry that discipleship is compromised. Leadership through spiritual gifts, however, brings not only vitality to a congregation but also produces faithful discipleship. When Christians discover their spiritual gifts, they discern the self they are meant to be.

CHAPTER 2

DIRECTIONS

Charlene volunteered for duties at the church office shortly after joining St. Paul's. She quickly demonstrated capacity for a significant volume of work. She also knew the importance of accuracy in details. With growing insight, she sensed both member and prospective member needs. She helped us match those needs with appropriate persons and resources.

Within a short period, she became a volunteer care coordinator for the congregation. She gave a few hours each week. She followed up on posthospitalization needs in homes where new babies arrived, and with families experiencing loss through death. Her administrative oversight guided pastoral and membership care in new directions. Her penchant for detail ensured that few congregational needs fell through the cracks. The fruits of her work affected the morale of the congregation. They sensed a new level of responsiveness from their church.

A suggestion surfaced regarding a part-time staff position in membership care. The need and the fruits of such a position were clear. However, costs were prohibitive. The money was simply not available. A member family offered a one-year "challenge gift" to fund the position. After one year, the fruits of the position would need to be self-evident and, thus, self-supporting. Charlene was employed part-time. She brought energy and supervision to this segment of our ministry. The position was easily funded the next year. The church grew *toward* her gifts and *as a result* of her gifts. Additional spiritual gifts emerged *because* of her gifts. Her spiritual gifts matched a growing need in a growing church. Those gifts helped us define an area of ministry in an unexpected way.

Ephesians 4:11-12 is God's working design for the local church. This fragment of Scripture proves to be *the definitive working description* of the church in capsule form. What if every church took these words as a tiny mustard seed to be planted? Is it possible that an exciting, dynamic, relational ministry could grow from a full devotion to these words?

God gives each member of the believing community certain gifts. Exactly how and when the gifts are given, we do not know. Perhaps at Christian baptism as we are welcomed into the family of faith? Perhaps not until the time of confirmation or the public affirmation of one's faith? Perhaps the complete blossoming of God's spiritual gifts does not manifest itself until middle adulthood. *When* we receive our gifts, and the *manifestation* of those gifts, differs for each individual.

What About "Talents"?

Fifteen years ago, Linda was a volunteer director of one children's choir. She was quiet, but effective in using her musical training. She also sang regularly with the adult choir. When the diaconal minister of music left the church for a new position, Linda was asked to "fill in temporarily" during a search process. Within a few months, it was obvious that God had given her special gifts in music leadership. The temporary position became permanent. Her talents broadened. New, unexpected gifts emerged.

Today, the choir ministry encompasses a growing number of singers, children's choir parent guilds, and special concerts. The sanctuary is often filled to capacity for musical offerings under her direction. She is now a consecrated diaconal minister of music. Clearly, God redefined her innate talent. Spiritual gifts germinated, grew, and flowered.

A thoughtful skeptic or psychologist will ask the inevitable question about "talents." Are "talents" and "spiritual gifts" discernibly different? A distinction can be made. While some talents may be nurtured by God and then transformed, spiritual gifts manifest themselves through our personhood in unique ways.

Various biblical texts in the letters to the churches strongly suggest that spiritual gifts are received from outside the individual's effort: they are outright gifts of the Holy Spirit. "*To each is given* the manifestation of the

Spirit for the common good" (1 Cor. 12:7, *emphasis mine*). Some spiritual gifts may come from God's blessing upon natural talents and skills. Others seem to be direct gifts with no prior indication.[1]

Ephesians 4:11-12 suggests that we can only be pastors (caregivers), Christian teachers (imparting some understanding of the faith and Scriptures), prophets (interpreters of God's time and purpose), or preachers (apostles, witnesses to the Resurrection) as God gives us the suitable spiritual gifts. The expression of a full life suggests that each of us ought to utilize our talents as much as possible. But the "abundant life" which Jesus offered (see John 10:10) requires a more holistic perspective. We must be open to the transformation of our talents as well as being sensitive to the unexpected emergence of spiritual gifts.

Rich retired early as a public school chemistry teacher with a "secret love" for mechanical things. He restores old cars as a hobby, and he is fascinated with sophisticated mechanical operations. I was prompted to approach him about the need for a building maintenance supervisor when the position opened on our staff. He looked at me in wonder. "This must be an answer to prayer. I have been looking for something like this in my life," he said. "I have asked God to use me in a fresh way." In a few short months, he became an invaluable part of his church's ministry. His talents and skills were retooled into spiritual gifts by the active grace of a divine Presence.

Much of the energy of spiritual gift development is akin to the work of a symphony or choral conductor. Each member of the body has a talent to offer. However, the director combines the best in each individual. Together they create beautiful music.

Limitations of the Charismatic Movement

Early in my ministry, the charismatic movement seemed to be a dominant force everywhere I turned. Charismatic prayer groups, business groups, Bible study groups, healing groups, "full gospel" fellowships, and home meetings sprang up everywhere. Not infrequently, Christian friendships were strained to a breaking point—including a few of my own—over this issue. Judgments were passed concerning one's eternal destiny on the basis of speaking in tongues.

Upon occasion, narrowly defined spiritual gifts would make their way into the staid and ordered flow of mainline Protestant worship. Such expressions caused confusion, misunderstanding, and distrust. The events sometimes splintered existing congregations.

Speaking in tongues *is* one demonstration of the Spirit. As a form of prayer and praise toward God, it can be a beautiful gift. For many, however, this manifestation of the Holy Spirit has been the sole emphasis regarding spiritual gifts.

My personal commitment is to a much broader ecclesiology of spiritual gifts. Such a commitment grew out of theological struggle as well as a desire to express what I have gradually realized to be true. *Spiritual gifts are major building blocks for the creation of a strong congregation.*

While some specific manifestations of the Spirit (such as speaking in tongues) are appropriate in the life of the church, they should not be the primary focus for a full theology of spiritual gifts. Such a notion is too limiting because it attempts to stabilize the unexpected flow of God's gifts for ministry. Any such boundary is also inadequate to the biblical witness. The marvelous gifts to which the Ephesians text refers are more broadly based. Multiple gifts are indigenous and unique to every congregation.

A variety of spiritual gifts are named throughout various New Testament letters.[2] None of the lists is exhaustive. The consistent implication is that each of us is given one or more of these gifts. Some are traditional (e.g., preaching and teaching). Some may occasion controversy (e.g., healing or prophecy). Some seem relevant only to the first century. Some may yet be revealed as gifts for the next century.[3]

Fresh Terminology

Two mice went for an early morning stroll. As they rounded a corner, they came face-to-face with a hungry cat. As the cat prepared to pounce, one of the mice *barked* at the cat. The cat was so startled that he turned and ran. Whereupon the mouse said to his companion, "In times like these, it's nice to know a second language!"

Ephesians 4:11-12 provides us with a useful second language with which to address the church's ministry. Gifts of the Spirit are for a *twofold* purpose: (1) the work of ministry and (2) building up the Body of Christ (Eph. 4:12). The work of ministry is the *outreach* of the church. The building up of the body is the *inreach*.[4] The first is missional and involves action in the world; the second is personal and concerns the inner life of the believer. Both are indispensable to the life of faith. Each is dependent upon the presence of the other.

An appropriate symbol for this is the geometric form of the ellipse. The ellipse is an oblong circle with two focal points instead of one.

SKETCH OF AN ELLIPSE HERE

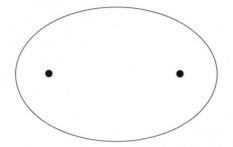

The two focal points relate to the circumference of the ellipse by a mathematical equation. In order for the figure to retain its shape, these two points must remain in proper balance. If either becomes displaced, the ellipse immediately loses symmetry.

So it is with the church. *There must be a healthy balance between two main thrusts: inreach and outreach.* Some examples of inreach ministries are:

Corporate worship: the energizing event out of which other forms of growth and discipleship emerge.

Sacred hymns and songs of faith: nurturing the soul and giving expression to our joys and sorrows.

Bible study and devotional reading: providing insight and direction. We touch the pilgrimage of faith's forebears. We learn how others experience God.

Prayer: learning to pray. Some form of daily prayer, even "prayer on the run," sustains the soul. Prayer keeps us in touch with the Eternal.

Communion: Many spiritual gifts come alive when the sacrament is regularly offered to the people of God. The best design is frequent opportunity for communion in a variety of settings. Communion is also an appropriate expression for the gift of healing.[5]

Covenant Discipleship Groups: a more recent inreach offering. The format is one hour weekly with five to seven other persons. Each member is accountable for an agreed covenant of Christian discipline. Covenant Discipleship has deeply affected my own life in recent years.

If the Christian life is to retain its balance, however, there must also be opportunities for works of outreach. Some examples of outreach ministries are:

Works of compassion and mercy: care for the elderly, food and clothing for the hungry and naked, shelter for the homeless, and emergency resources for those caught in sudden disasters.

Works of justice: advocating for children and the elderly; opposing systems that perpetuate racism; combating those forces that destroy the life God intends (e.g., gambling, alcohol abuse, family violence, and encroaching secularization).

Alternative giving habits: giving gifts that sustain the earth; purchasing gifts that assist those in developing sections of the world; exercising less consumptive patterns.

Adult day care: weekday care where the growing numbers of older adults needing care can find meaning in the closing years of life. Such ministries also provide some much needed respite for the caregivers themselves.

Child care: preschool programs, mother's day out, drop-in child care, and full day care (including latchkey and "second shift" care).

One fall, both major public school districts in our area suffered a long and bitter strike. Recognizing the emotional impact this event has upon children and their families, we began a ministry of intercessory prayer for all parties. As an outgrowth of that prayer time, a group of staff and lay volunteers organized an "Until School Starts" ministry at the church. This ministry of outreach provided structured time and activity for nearly two hundred elementary age children for six weeks.

Staff leadership offered the gifts of planning and resources. Volunteer laity brought gifts of time, energy, support, and innovative ideas. They also cheerfully provided funding to cover costs. Those six weeks rendered emotional health to families and made an important statement to the community about the role of the Christian church. During the entire time, "Until School Starts" continued to be undergirded with prayer. Even in this short-term ministry, *inreach and outreach maintained an appropriate balance.*

If a congregation is built only upon inreach ministries, members become inward and self-serving. If a congregation is only doing outreach, the church may become bereft of the spiritual energy needed to meet the challenges of a complex world. The pendulum has swung in both extremes in the recent history of the church in North America.

The writer of Ephesians knew nothing about the mathematical intricacies of the ellipse. Yet, he offers a model for the Christian congregation that speaks profoundly to that image. *The gifts of the Holy Spirit are given in order to ensure a healthy, balanced life of faithful discipleship.* God calls the church to a sustained, steady symmetry between inreach and outreach. God gives gifts to nourish this balance.

The Wesleyan Tradition

John Wesley lived and preached a balanced "elliptical" ministry. He was concerned simultaneously with the salvation of souls *and* the education of the poor. He was an advocate for methodical spiritual discipline *and* an opponent of liquor traffic. He preached about obedience in fasting and prayer *and* he took strong exception to the slave trade of his time. He modeled a healthy rhythm between the two poles. He was given spiritual gifts to exercise leadership in both dimensions. He called others to the exercise of these gifts as well.

While Wesley never seemed to prioritize these two poles of ministry, he *did* suggest that the works of spiritual growth (inreach) might come more easily to a Christian than the works of compassion, mercy, and justice (outreach). He suggested, therefore, that we consider the works of outreach first—not because they were more important, but because they might otherwise be neglected.

The most common renderings of the text in Ephesians 4:12 seem to make this same emphasis. The *Good News* translation reads, "He did this to prepare all God's people for the work of Christian service, [and] . . . to build up the body of Christ." When "Christian service" suggests outreach, and "building up the body" suggests inreach, the emphases are clear. The NRSV translation is essentially the same. Outreach is considered "first," only because it requires more intentionality by most of us within the Christian community.

The search for specific spiritual gifts for outreach ministries deserves balanced priority in a local church agenda. When leaders give extra attentiveness to signals in this direction for their congregation, they will find a new vitality in ministry. The wisdom of Wesley is appropriate to all congregations and denominations.

Centered in the Holy Spirit

A man was employed by the highway department to paint a center line in the middle of a road. The first day, he painted two miles. The boss was very pleased. The second day he painted one mile. The boss was curious, but still pleased. The third day the man only painted about 100 feet. The boss was *not* pleased. "What's going on here?" asked the boss. The man replied, "Each day I find that I am farther and farther from the bucket."

The leadership design of any church must not get too far from the Holy Spirit. Fully developed discipleship of inreach and outreach demands a strong dependence upon the work of the Spirit. The gifts that God gives to believers are a manifestation of the work of the Spirit. Any church that desires a balanced ministry, therefore, is one where the people have some convictions regarding the work of the Holy Spirit.

Such an emphasis is not always easy. The term "Holy Spirit" makes some Christians uneasy and wary. While we long for a deeper spiritual dimension to life, we are not always comfortable with discussions regarding the Holy Spirit. If Ephesians 4:11-12 is to be taken seriously, we must reacquaint ourselves with the Spirit in our midst. We must also know and articulate the impact of the Spirit in our daily life.

The Failure of the Model in Church History

From the beginning of Christian history, the church was founded as a laity-centered movement. As congregations were established, the gifts of the people were called forth and utilized in that place. Clergy overseers (including elders and bishops) were early *additions* to the local organization, growing out of the life of the total church. The real work of ministry (care for widows and orphans, tending to the spiritual needs of the sick, basic instruction, and probably considerable preaching) were the work of deacons and the lay church members. The apostles and others moved in a wide geographical area proclaiming and interpreting the Resurrection.

Presumably, bishops and elders became leaders and overseers for a larger town or region.

By the third or fourth century, most of the decision making and pastoral oversight of the church gravitated into the hands of professionals. One cannot be absolutely certain what caused this change. Perhaps, positions of leadership in these early Christian congregations shifted toward a few powerful individuals in each region. Ruling elders or a monarchical episcopate may have emerged in this way. Apparently the laity let it happen. A great treasure of local church vitality disappeared. Authority and the practice of ministry through a human hierarchy became dominant.

Periodically, attempts were made to restore the gift of basic ministry to the laity of the church. Martin Luther raised the notion of the "priesthood of all believers." While Luther gave important theological grounding to the movement, he never set a particular plan in motion.

John Wesley initiated an organizational movement in eighteenth-century England. Wesley arranged believers into classes and appointed class leaders. He assigned certain lay men and women to preach in "Methodist" pulpits on regular occasions. In part, the genius of the Wesleyan movement was the reawakening of the power of the laity.

When the church came to America, the frontier was rough and hazardous. Circuit riders could only reach villages and towns irregularly. Much of the work of ministry was still carried out by lay men and women who remained on-site. However, as the frontier settled, so did the preachers. They became residents within the communities instead of "traveling elders." Once more, the reins of leadership and pastoral care passed to the clergy, *and the laity let it happen.* Some of this may have been an unconscious trend, but it gradually eroded the dynamism of the church.

We need laity who know and believe that they have real gifts from God. We need lay men and women who discern and trust the promptings of the Holy Spirit without apprehension or misgivings. We need clergy who will oversee those gifts and who affirm the presence of God's Spirit on behalf on the Kingdom. To do so will restore encouragement and joy to the local church.

One clergy overseer, in clarifying the ministry of spiritual gifts to his congregation after some personal rediscovery, wrote:

> Christians are encouraged to discover their God-given spiritual gift. They are not expected to rotate from position to position or committee to committee. Instead they are set free to develop the creative gift God has

given them. In many cases they will stay with one or two gifts all of their lifetime and thus become an expert who can train others who have the same gift. New leaders are discovered based on how they serve rather than how faithfully they function in a meeting. Robert's Rules of Order are replaced by the passion to serve in some area of ministry. People with administrative skills serve on committees; extroverted people work with people; people who love to teach and have that gift, teach. *Very few people burn out!* Instead, they find meaning and purpose for their lives as well as build up the body of Christ.

He concluded with this personal confession: "Frankly, I am embarrassed that for the past 23 years this major emphasis in the New Testament has gone unnoticed in my ministry."[6]

My hope is that such an emphasis will not continue unnoticed. Spiritual giftedness should become essential to doing ministry into the twenty-first century. The specific suggestions in ensuing chapters will provide resources to that end.

CHAPTER 3

CLAIMING TRADITIONAL GIFTS

M y father was an active layman in the local church all of his adult life. Consistently faithful with his presence and financial support, he was frequently asked to lead committees or even make an occasional statement in public worship. He confided to me that he always felt uncomfortable in the public eye. His gifts were elsewhere.

As a trained and experienced civil engineer, he provided valuable know-how in areas of construction, maintenance, mechanical systems, and business operations. Only occasionally were his true gifts perceived during his most active years. After taking early retirement from government work at age 58, he became the business administrator in a large church. Actually, his specialty was as a facilities administrator.

He served that church in his own quiet but invaluable way. His pastor spoke of these matters at his memorial service: "His gifts for this task in the church were quite remarkable." His spiritual gifts had finally been accurately discerned. He lived as a mostly private person with exceptional gifts to deploy for his Lord through the church.

On any given Sunday morning, a congregation laden with emotions, problems, and life experiences arrives for worship. A sensitive and caring worship leader knows worshipers who are hurting, lonely, anxious, unable to forgive, and needing forgiveness. Alternatively, that same leader sees worshipers who are full of joy, personal satisfaction, and fulfilled expectations. Members and visitors appear—uneasy and rejoicing, in fear and in awe, discouraged and hopeful. They arrive plagued with doubts and blessed with assurance.

However, *the most important dynamic* in any gathered congregation is a beautiful array of spiritual gifts. Those who gather for worship have varieties of gifts that can be used for ministry. God has prepared these gifts as instruments of the Kingdom.

Many congregations produce pictorial directories every few years. Such directories are helpful tools for ministry. They put names to faces. However, these pictorial directories also serve another important function. They become instruments of prayer and meditation regarding the spiritual gifts of those appearing on each page. Beyond the ordinary function, directories serve as opportunities to see persons through the eyes of the Spirit.

If pastors are perplexed about low commitment and plateaued attendance, then an urgent need exists to reacquaint congregations with the concept of spiritual gifts. The most important skill for an ordained church leader is the discernment to recognize these gifts from God in others.

Is this not what Jesus did when he called the disciples? They were fishermen, tax collectors, and others from assorted backgrounds. None were community leaders. They were common folk called to an uncommon task that directly changed the course of human history.

Undoubtedly, Jesus saw the gifts before he saw the individual. Later, the disciples and other apostles (challenged by the emerging theology of Paul) became primary identifiers of spiritual gifts within the community of faith. Perhaps this is where the New Testament term "overseer" originated.[1] The spiritual leaders of the earliest congregations visualized their flock from a distinct vantage point. They saw beyond themselves toward the potential of others.

Every clergy leader needs to practice this skill of discernment among God's people. Many believers have simply never been told about God's design for the church. They have never been assisted in recognizing spiritual gifts. They remain unable to identify spiritual gifts in themselves or in others.

Many contemporary Christians simply do not believe they are gifted. They protest the theology of spiritual gifts. They humbly object: "This is a very talented congregation, pastor. But I don't really have any special gifts at all." Or, "This is a very small church, pastor. There cannot be many gifts in this crowd!" Such posturing by even one church member not only is unfortunate but it is also incorrect. The faithful of every congregation need to learn the way God intends the church to thrive.

We believe that God is always ready to offer some great work through the gifts of the Christian community. This attitude generates a sense of hope that God's work will lead to more excellent results through the gifts found in the next generation of believers. That expectant attitude is revealed in the story of a little girl who was sitting with her grandfather in her room. "Grandpa," she began, "Did God make you?"

"Yes, child," came the reply. "God made me."

After a pause, the girl asked, "And Grandpa, did God make me too?" Again, the answer was affirmative. She looked in the mirror for a while and then said, "You know, Grandpa, God is doing a whole lot better work lately."

The principles of redundancy and repetition are indispensable to assist in the process of gift discovery in the church. Members learn how to celebrate their gifts through upbeat, clear, and varied input about spiritual gifts. You are a child of God. God's grace has bestowed upon you certain spiritual gifts. Look within, claim, and use those gifts! Pray and listen for the call. To what is God calling you?

Initial Preparation

A few years ago, I began using some of the resources and techniques from a small group facilitator in an initial attempt to improve the perception regarding spiritual gifts in members. The material is well-suited to both youth and adults.[2]

For example, a retreat event might close with an exercise called "gift giving." Having spent time together, the group sits in a large circle. One person then walks to a chair in the center of the circle. Members of the group engage in "gift giving" or "gift bombardment"—naming those special gifts of God discovered in that person.

Such gift-giving can provide uplifting closing worship. The moments of gift bombardment provide a powerful spiritual experience. High school youth work through the experience eagerly and well. They name the gifts and celebrate the naming process with enthusiasm. Adults occasionally have a bit more difficulty breaking free from inhibitions. But the total experience is always a "building up" time for those who take part. After repeating the process in various group constellations, the reality of widespread spiritual gifts begins to come alive in clusters of members. They tell "stories" about their particular retreat experience and discovery. The enthusiasm can be contagious.

A modified version of the gift-giving process can be utilized in new member orientation. The clergy leader or other facilitator presents a theology and ecclesiology of spiritual gifts to the group, using Ephesians 4:11-12 as a framework. After lifting up the specific gifts in that text, other contemporary gifts are added by way of illustration. Gift examples should be visible ones as well as gifts that exist behind the scenes. The examples should also draw on images familiar to persons who have only been with the congregation for a short time period.

Visible gifts could be those of greeters, ushers, parking lot attendants, Sunday school teachers, or choir members. Less visible gifts might be those of the altar guild, bulletin assembly crews, offering counters, telephone receptionists, or computer data entry volunteers.

After presenting some illustrations, allow the group a moment to reflect on these gifts. Often, they experience the first new awareness that they are gifted people by God's grace. The group divides into smaller units. Smiles of recognition break through, and animated conversation ensues. Each individual suggests to a few others where they *might* see themselves in the life of the congregation in the next few years.

A minister went to call in the home of a young family. The six-year-old son answered the door. While waiting for the mother to enter the room, the two struck up a conversation. "Well, young man," said the minister, "what do you want to be when you grow up?"

The child responded, "Possible."

The minister responded, "I don't quite understand. What do you mean?"

Came the reply, "Well, just about every day my mom tells me I'm impossible! So I want to be possible when I grow up."

All Christians are God's gifted possibilities. This anticipation of varied gifts is a primary cause of the joy of receiving new persons into the ministry and mission of the congregation.

Special gifts await identification, naming, calling forth, training, and implementation. In several new member classes, I discovered an able board chairperson, a hunger coordinator, junior high Sunday school teachers, and a couple who are giving leadership to a membership care commission.

Very little coaching is needed from the pastor/overseer. For some—newer Christians and long term church members alike—it may be the first time they have been prodded to think in terms of spiritual gifts. Later, when preaching or teaching reinforces the theology, newer members are already acquainted with the concepts and terminology.

The fundamental principle of spiritual gifts undergirding the local church is this: *there are sufficient gifts in every congregation to do what God is calling that congregation to do.* This statement encompasses both an affirmation of faith and an intellectual conviction. Whether your congregation is 50, 500, or 5,000 members, the principle applies. As such, the matter is a primary tenet of Christian doctrine and the indisputable witness of the biblical record. The principle of spiritual gifts is not dependent upon the administrative qualifications of the leader. Clergy and laity alike are surprised by joy when engaged in the process.

Preparation of the Leader

Leadership through spiritual gifts is strengthened through Bible study. Personal reflection and the literature of leadership is also important. Continuing education or a short study leave provides helpful preparation and grounding. The subject deserves one's undivided attention, away from daily routine and duties. Initiating leadership and continued development of leadership through spiritual gifts needs concentrated energy and thought.[3]

A group of laypersons can become a valuable sounding board for the ordained leader. They function as an unofficial gift design team, which is not formally introduced into the structure of the church. Such a group can support the emerging process with prayer, thoughtful insight, and critical review from varied perspectives.

Select six to eight persons, each willing to do some minimal reading. They may offer counsel regarding the particular leadership qualities of the clergy. They can assess how those qualities will match their particular congregation. Sessions with this group need not be more often than every other month. The fruits of the process will undoubtedly provide many occasions for new appreciation of the work of the church.

While there are workbooks and workshops available on this subject, I prefer a less structured style.[4] Clergy and laity should develop a method-ology that is suited to the clergy's leadership style and the characteristics of the congregation. If the church is to move in this direction, ownership must be instilled from the beginning.

The clergy leader should preach regularly on some aspect of the ecclesiology of spiritual gifts. Installation of church officers, recognition of church school teachers, and confirmation are appropriate settings for such messages. Brief illustrations in the church's newsletter using the language of spiritual gifts also heighten congregational awareness. Members and nonjoiners begin to assimilate the language into their own vocabulary. The transitory nature of our society requires that we repeat this theology of the church regularly.

One of the great joys of ministry is hearing unsolicited comments regarding the utilization of spiritual gifts. When laity begin to live the concept, they share it with others. They exhibit a genuine sense of ownership.

Margie has worked with me in the new member assimilation process for more than a decade. Her innate ability for greeting, welcoming, and remembering important details of persons' lives has been a joy to discover and encourage. Her capacity for this is quite extraordinary. As we continue to develop a working theology of spiritual gifts, Margie has also discovered her gift for "seeing" gifts in others. She has become a primary resource for placing persons where their gifts apply. New members regularly ask, "How does she do it?"

I reply, "Discerning and naming your gifts is *her* gift!"

Lay Pastoral Care: A Place to Begin

Jayne was assigned her first contact as a lay pastor for the church. Having completed two months of the training, she was nervous but eager to begin. She was assigned to a member who had lost her elderly mother in recent weeks. The woman, who was relatively new to the congregation, spoke with an accent that strained communication.

Jayne's journal recorded her first visit with descriptive imagery, loaded with feelings. She read it to the other lay pastors-in-training: "I sat in my car for the longest time, trying to muster my courage. Finally, I got out of the car and walked toward the door. I put my finger to the doorbell with heart pounding and knees shaking. I had no idea what I would say. But I knew that God continued in this with me. I was doing something for which God had called and equipped me."

Ephesians 4:11 says, "The gifts [God] gave were that some would be apostles, some prophets, some evangelists, some *pastors.*" The designation *pastors* for the earliest church referred to the laity. The pastors of the early church were *not* the apostles, *not* the clergy leaders, but *rather* the laity of the church. The laity were the instruments of the basic ongoing pastoral needs of the people. Apostles and skilled preachers were in short supply. They could not spread the good news while at the same time providing day-to-day care for the young churches. Therefore, lay pastors offered the basic work of routine care while the apostles and other gifted leaders moved from town to town with the resurrection message.

Reclaiming pastoral care by laity is an excellent place to introduce the ecclesiology of spiritual gifts. Congregations might not immediately accept lay pastors—and a few denominational overseers might be hesitant about the implications for word, order, and sacrament—but continued efforts will produce results.

Ronald Sunderland teaches that pastoral ministry by the laity can transform congregational care in revitalizing ways.[5] The biblical model for pastors from Ephesians 4:11-12 is especially relevant in our time.

According to Sunderland's design, laypeople do the basic, continuing pastoral care, under the supervision of the ordained clergy. Lay pastors who care for the body are a supplement to—but do not lessen responsibility for—caregiving through the work of the clergy. They bring their spiritual gifts for caring and listening to lonely, hurting people. The clergy are always present to members of the church and the extended church family. But a system of redundancy in lay pastoral care allows time for the clergy to improve other duties and seize new opportunities in connection with their call to ministry.

The most elemental plan for lay pastoral care calls for a wide variety of caregiving situations. Lay pastors are primarily generalists. One day, a lay pastor visits a new mother who is temporarily housebound with her infant. Another day, she visits a shut-in who needs to tell the story of her husband's lengthy illness one more time. On yet another day, her visit is made to a hospitalized church member who needs additional contact between the visits of the ordained clergy. She may also visit a grieving middle-aged woman who served as the primary caregiver through a lengthy illness of a favorite aunt. She has been trained as a good listener and caring presence.

The next step, however, goes beyond the practice of the generalist. As God reveals new gifts, lay pastors are called to specialized caring ministries. Spiritual gifts are refined within the ministry of lay pastoral care.

Some caregivers are particularly effective in hospital visitation and follow-up care for those who had surgery or serious illness. My wife, Elaine, spent three months in a hospital bed following a serious automobile accident. Pat received the assignment as her lay pastor. She came to the house regularly, always sensing the right duration for a visit. Each time, she brought a small gift: some fruit, an unusual food (broccoli coleslaw!), a card, or a small book. She simply sat by the bed—talking, listening, or remaining appropriately silent. When I needed to be away overnight, Pat immediately offered to spend the night in our home. She exemplified the gifted, well trained, pleasant lay pastor during those difficult months.

Some lay pastors are especially helpful in grief work. They visit a family at the funeral home. They attend the funeral or memorial service. They bring systematic follow-up in the homes of the grieving family for an extended time after the ordained pastor has moved on to other care crises.

At a memorial service for an elderly parishioner, scarcely a dozen persons were present. The deceased had no children, and only a distant extended family. However, one of the persons attending was a young woman from the congregation. She entered the room just as the service was beginning. She seemed almost out of place. After the service ended, I walked up to her and said, "Katie, I am delighted to see you. It is good that you could come."

"Oh," she replied softly, "I enjoyed visiting as his lay pastor." She proceeded to tell me of his long rambling stories about his marriage, and his wealth of knowledge regarding several rural counties in southwestern Pennsylvania—stories that I had also heard over the years of our acquaintance and visits. She extended a listening, caring presence for him over many months. She came to the memorial service as an expression of closure for one who had become a friend.

Some lay pastors are particularly effective with shut-ins, willing to listen to a lot of repeated stories of personal history. They have time to make frequent visits. They can bring little gifts of cheer: flowers, fruit, a magazine. They can provide respite for the caregivers. Such visits require time and attention that the clergy are frequently unable to give. The fruits of specialized lay pastoral care in local church ministry are obvious. As generalists, lay pastors enhance the ministry of the church. But when they begin to specialize, they experience a deep personal satisfaction in their call from God. The "fruit of the Spirit" (Gal. 5:22) develop more fully. Lay pastoral care is occurring all the time in the church. We witness the ministry in Sunday school classes, women's circles, Bible study groups, choirs, coffee hours, and similar settings. However, such caring is informal and unsupervised. The time has come for the church to tap this resource of spiritual gifts and use lay pastors in a more purposeful ministry, which extends the web of influence that a congregation provides.

How are lay pastors called out of the congregation? As members demonstrate the gift for caring and listening in the life of the congregation, their endowment is recognized by others. The most effective procedure for building a team of lay pastors is *invitation*. Gifts are discerned and called out. Lay pastors are not usually self-selecting volunteers.

To initiate the process, a letter is sent inviting an individual to consider this form of congregational caregiving. The letter is followed by a personal contact by the clergy leader. (Some congregations may assign this visitation to a volunteer leader who is organizing the lay pastors in ministry, but without direct clergy involvement, the structure is less likely to be sustained.) Specific information is provided regarding the ministry and the reason for selecting this man or woman.

A training process follows. Special needs among the elderly, the hospitalized, the bereaved, and others are examined. Certain basic skills are taught—removing one's coat on a visit so as to suggest plenty of time, sitting down beside a hospital bed, phrases to open conversation—each skill giving the lay pastors more confidence. Sessions on "stages of grief" and basic listening skills are also presented. Role-playing sessions help to hone those skills. Occasionally, training utilizes generic verbatims adapted from actual visits.[6]

The training process is flexible. Most lay pastoral gifts develop as visits are made. Participation in the training process does not require that the person become a lay pastor. Should the person not feel called to this ministry, other options for using spiritual gifts can be explored. To decline the call to lay pastoral ministry is not to "fail" or "drop out." Rather, it is grounds to examine a different utilization of one's spiritual gifts.

A new class of lay pastors should be trained at least once each calendar year. Once the ministry is in place, lay pastors become an excellent resource for naming and identifying others who might have the same gifts. Lay pastors are asked to list persons whom they would like to see invited into the ministry. The various lists are compared. The same name(s) on several lists indicates an appropriate identification of this pastoral gift.

Occasionally, the clergy might ask the congregation for suggestions: "Whom do you see as a very caring listener in this church family?" Use a bulletin insert or other response form. Trust the laity to recognize God's work in others. The assumption should never be made that clergy are the only persons who can identify gifts that are being sought.

Lay pastors are assigned as needed. The assignments are in accordance with the number of persons each lay pastor feels he or she can sustain at a given time. Lay pastors become a prominent part of congregational care. They provide continuity and depth. They are an extension of the clergy presence for the congregation.

A further development with lay pastoral care concerns the sacrament of communion. Lay pastors take consecrated communion elements to the sick and shut-ins during a worship hour on Sunday morning. While the gathered congregation comes to the Table, those who cannot be present receive the sacrament at home or in a hospital room. Although some denominational traditions may find this procedure inappropriate, it does seem in keeping with biblical tradition. Such distribution is always monitored and supervised by an ordained elder.[7]

Lay pastoral care frees the clergy for the utilization of his or her call to word, order, and sacrament. The ordained clergy retain very important roles within the congregation. They continue to work in crisis intervention, make hospital calls, and respond at the time of a death. They generally become less involved in *long-term* convalescent care, *extended* periods of bereavement, and *frequent* shut-in visitation. Some decisions about visits by the ordained clergy are made at the suggestion of the lay pastor. Clergy oversee the lay pastors in systematic fashion. Lay pastors meet monthly with the ordained clergy for support, guidance, prayer, and monitoring of assignments.

Two unexpected blessings flow from lay pastoral care. First, the congregation experiences a definite sense of being well cared for. When good clergy oversight is in place, and when lay pastoral care is operative, fewer persons have cause to complain that "nobody ever came" or "nobody ever called." During the past five years in my own congregation, I cannot recall a single instance of complaint regarding lack of care in the congregational life. *I am convinced that this is primarily due to regular lay pastoral visitation throughout the church family.*

A second blessing: lay pastors sense their participation in genuine ministry. *Lay pastors believe they are making a difference in people's lives.* Here is ministry with a purpose, one that has a durable impact. Occasionally, they may know themselves as instruments of therapeutic treatment or spiritual transformation. They sense that they are involved in the work of Christ. This is precisely the way in which spiritual gifts are meant to affect the Christian community.

The biblical texts are clear. These texts offer ample opportunities for preaching and education. Some early objections to lay pastoral care may arise.[8] Such objections dissipate within a few months. The hearts of the congregation are easily won for this ministry, regardless of initial doubts.

Teachers in the Sunday School

David and Mary joined the church several years ago. David navigates the world in a motorized wheelchair after a swimming accident. They adopted two Peruvian children and brought them for Christian baptism soon after legal issues were finalized. Each Sunday morning, David and Mary arrive with their children twenty minutes before the Sunday school hour. Together, they team-teach a young children's Sunday school class. In the midst of personal struggle coupled with a busy home life, they have become gifted and committed teachers in the Sunday school. Their witness to the children is extraordinary.

Ephesians 4:11 names *teachers* as one of the gifts of the Spirit. Thus, a second area for initiating the theology of spiritual gifts is the recruitment of leadership teams or teachers for the Sunday school.

Typically, Sunday school superintendents and directors of Christian education suffer annual "August anxiety attacks" when they approach recruitment for the ensuing year. How many churches have experienced the following scenario? About August 15, there is a knock at the door of the minister's study. It is the Sunday school superintendent or director of Christian education. "Pastor, we've got a serious problem. I cannot find anyone to teach the third grade Sunday school class this year. I've tried *everyone* I know, and no one is willing to take on this class. What should we do? Can you ask for volunteers this Sunday in church?"

Dutifully, the pastor uses all his or her persuasive powers the following Sunday. "OK, friends, we have a problem. As of now, we don't have a teacher for the third grade children. Unless we can find someone in the next two weeks, *there will be no third grade Sunday school class this year.* Is anyone here able to help? Can we find a volunteer? It is urgent!" The congregation squirms.

After the service, a long-time member approaches the minister. "I'll do it, Reverend. We can't let the children down. I'll teach the third grade." Her voice sounds tired. The tone is one of obvious reluctance. But the minister gives a sigh of relief—for himself and for the congregation.

Such a scenario utilizes guilt instead of gifts. It is emotional arm twisting to get the job done. It is unworthy of the Church of Jesus Christ because it will often backfire in the classroom.

Consider this alternative: a small group of those committed to teaching children in the church gathers in the minister's study in mid-June. The list of "openings" is reviewed by someone in the group. Teachers and coleaders are needed for about five different classes by September. The first vacancy is that of the third grade.

The minister or director of Christian education begins with the question: "If you could put the very best person you know into the third grade class, who would it be?" No concern is expressed at this point about how busy the person might be, or whether that person might respond affirmatively. Who is the *best person*? Who has gifts for relating to third graders?

Names begin to surface. Perhaps two, perhaps five or six. Now the leader asks a new question: "Help me prioritize this list. Who is the top choice of this group? Who is *the most gifted person* to work with third graders on this list?" After considerable reflection, a prioritized list emerges.

The group pauses to pray over the list of names they have developed. The minister (or education chairperson) writes a letter to the first person on the list. The letter in capsule form, reads something like this:

Dear _____,

A group of us from First Church have been meeting concerning the needs of the Sunday School for the fall. After careful prayer and reflection, we believe that you are the person who has the gifts and graces for teaching the third graders of our congregation beginning in September.

You will, of course, receive training and support if you agree to serve in this way. Please commit this matter to prayer. _____ _____, our Education Committee chairperson, will contact you in a few days to ascertain your response.

Gratefully,

_____

The Spirit often moves the "top choices" to respond "yes." Persons willingly volunteer *without feeling manipulated or obligated.* They are pleased to know that others perceive gifts in them. They are willing to use those gifts for the task.

A second approach allows members of the congregation to "nominate" teachers for the ensuing year. A nominating form appears in the worship guide for several weeks in the late spring. Members are invited to suggest persons whom they believe have the gift of teaching. The names are collected and multiple nominations are noted. Prayers are offered. Teachers are recruited *because members have seen spiritual gifts in them!*

Sunday school teachers need to know that they are not expected to be experts on the Scriptures, theology, or church history. Rather, they need to love children. They also understand a bit about faith formation in young lives. They need to have some awareness of the characteristics of the particular age level they will teach.

Calling forth gifts in this way must include ample training and support. Expressions of appreciation are also important. A service of acknowledgment and appreciation each year is one way to recognize the "gift of teaching." Periodic notes of gratitude sent from the clergy leader and other staff offer support of their work. A teacher recognition dinner further values their endeavors. All of the above are ways to celebrate gifts in the lives of a very special group of people in your church.

The process is not difficult and it is usually far less time consuming than other methods. Most important, the process has theological and ecclesiological integrity. It can even be fun. It works! Church members learn something about spiritual gifts along the way. As always, a leader needs continuously to reexamine and refine the procedure. But God can and will use the process to accomplish divine purposes for the people of God.

The Nominating Committee

The work of the local church nominating committee can be a chore. Finding names and filling slots become a dull routine once each year. Negative feelings are amplified when calendar deadlines are imposed from on high. Occasional charges of power-brokering further deaden committee work. Selection for the nominating committee can be a dreaded event, even in the life of a stalwart church member. Transformation of the work of the nominating committee needs prompt attention.

Introduce the ecclesiology of spiritual gifts to the work of this committee! Here is a ready-made arena in which to explore the principles and the practice. Awareness of spiritual gifts can transform the nominating process. That same awareness can make the search for official leadership invigorating.

In some traditions, the pastor is automatically the chair of the committee on nominations. Occasionally, there may be an attempt to "control" who is in the elected offices of the church. While understanding the possibilities for "stacking" certain committees in the church, biblical leadership principles suggest that the ordained clergy *should* be the chairperson of nominations. As "overseer" of the life of the congregation, they are best-suited to provide spiritual leadership to this committee. Spiritual direction offered by a leader committed to the theology of spiritual gifts brings new energy to the task.

This committee's work is the heart of the theological task of identifying spiritual gifts of leadership within the body of believers. The work should not be seen as "filling empty slots." When the task is approached only as an organizational necessity, it becomes drudgery.

The committee on nominations needs to begin to ask new questions as they inaugurate their work each new season.

"Who can we get for this job?" becomes *"What gifts are necessary for this job?"*
"Where can _____ *and* _____ *serve this year?"* becomes *"Who has the gifts for this task?"*
"Who is a real worker around here?" becomes *"Who might God be calling to this task?"*

While sounding idealistic, these questions define the goal toward which to move.

Mark Twain reportedly once said, "Don't expect too much of human beings. We were created at the end of the week when God was tired and looking forward to a day off!" The church *deserves* high expectations of its nominating committee. Ask the hard questions! Believe that God will provide persons from the wealth of spiritual gifts bestowed upon the church! Trust the marvelous theology of a charismatic church.

Guard against "business as usual" in this task. Resist the old, familiar formats. Resist the human temptation to get the job done quickly and go home. When working on nominations, examine the process regularly. Each new nominating committee member must be trained in this format and its undergirding theology. As the committee becomes familiar with this approach, the entire process will be easier. The end result is worth the struggle.

After discerning the appropriate members for elected positions, the process continues by mail. A letter is mailed to each person who has been nominated. The letter describes the nominee's discerned gifts and indicates why they were selected for the particular position. A description of responsibilities and time commitments as well as the composition of the committee is also included.

Nominees are invited to pray about their response for a few days. They are urged to call the pastor or a person currently serving in that office if they have any questions. Finally, they are told that a specific individual from the nominating committee will call them in three or four days to ascertain their response. A copy of the letter goes to the committee member who will make the call, along with the home and work number of that individual.

When all positions have been filled, the nominees are duly elected by the appropriate church body. They should then be asked to present themselves for consecration at a Sunday morning service of worship. The service of consecration affirms the gifts of those elected, provides a call to commitment, and further educates the congregation.

Intercessory Prayer Groups

To pray is to resource ourselves in the energy of God's love. When we pray for others, we tap into that energy and become conduits for spiritual strength. Our prayers move in an arc through the heart of God to those for whom our prayers are offered. Intercessory prayer makes things happen—more things than we know! Those who give themselves to intercessory prayer are vital to the spiritual health of a congregation.

Jane gives a major segment of her life to prayer. Such activity seems to come naturally to her. When a small pilot intercessory group forms, she is part of the group. When the intercessory prayer and healing service convenes on Wednesday evening, she is there. During informal worship settings, when we ask for "names" of persons for whom to pray, Jane always contributes a name. When a time arrives in Sunday worship for intercessory prayer at the altar (during a prayer hymn) Jane is on her knees.

Some Christians seem to have a genuine call and a gift for prayer. In a few denominational traditions, these persons have been identified as "prayer warriors." Reclaiming intercessory prayer groups and prayer chains is long overdue in light of the theology of spiritual gifts.

How many of us have deferred the prayer ministry of the church to (1) the official pastoral prayer time in a service of worship or (2) the women's association or (3) a small group of spiritually faithful? Have we considered the vitality of a prayer ministry in the congregation that is rooted in the theology of spiritual gifts?

Prayer is a call of God in every Christian life. To be a disciple means to pray. Yet there are some persons who have a greater gift for prayer than others. Persons with such a gift not only keep you in "their thoughts," *they hold you in prayer.* When they make the statement, "I'll be praying for you," they are not being casual or merely polite. They *will* be praying for you!

In a recent conversation, a woman told me her concern regarding her position on a committee. She experienced difficulty finding a place on that committee. She voiced concern about the spiritual aspect of the group's decision-making process. "I am really praying about this," she told me, "but I am not comfortable making my apprehension known to the group."

After considerable discussion, I suggested, "Perhaps your primary role with this body is one of prayer support. Your primary gift may be to undergird their work with daily prayer." Her face came alive with a sense of new participation. She became a "prayer warrior" for the subsequent long months of deliberation and planning.

The church can be strengthened immeasurably by seeking those who have the gift of prayer. These individuals should be invited to use that gift on behalf of the congregation. Needs of the community and the world are appropriate as well.

A variety of settings for such prayer are appropriate. One common setting is a telephone prayer chain—carefully overseen by one who has a deep and loving commitment to prayer. This person must have the courage to nudge and call others. A second setting might be a weekly intercessory prayer group that meets for one hour. A third might be a midweek service of intercessory prayer for healing, followed by communion. A fourth option might be a prayer chapel or prayer room that is always open and available.

Individuals could be asked to pray daily for a specific issue before the congregation or the community. Training opportunities in intercessory prayer can be offered once or twice each year.[9] Let the whole congregation know that prayer is vital to the Christian experience, *but some have the gift of prayer.* Our people need to know how to pray. Some need to know how to use the calling to intercede in prayer as a gift from God. They are pleased to be asked to use their gift on behalf of the church. Other disciples who see this gift growing within themselves join them along the way.

Once again, the key is to discover those who feel called to pray. Affirm prayer as their gracious gift from God. They will know others who have the same gift. Sometimes those "others" are persons who are awkward or reticent about any public recognition of their gift. A church that mobilizes its gifted people for a prayer ministry will experience a surge of effective "elliptical" ministry. "The work of ministry" and the "building up of the Body of Christ"—outreach and inreach—will be in balance.

Summary

Four arenas for *beginning* a working theology of spiritual gifts are presented here. All four should probably not be introduced at one time. Any of the four can be a valuable teaching and learning experience. Whether developing lay pastors, nominating officers, recruiting teachers, building a prayer ministry, *or any other gift discernment,* the primary focus is the same. Spiritual gifts are present in God's people. These gifts only await being named, called forth, trained, and used in the life of the church.

Intentionally begun, a working theology of spiritual gifts will become more visible to members and growing disciples. Consequently, key words and phrases around "spiritual gifts" must be used at every opportunity. Small victories should be regularly celebrated.

Words of encouragement come regularly from the pulpit and pen of the "theologian in residence." In multiple staff situations, the entire leadership team works together to understand and implement the strategy of spiritual gifts.

Celebrate! Affirm! Explain! Teach and preach! Allow people to know the meaning of "spiritual gifts" and the relationship of those gifts to the Body of Christ.

As we prepared for a major capital campaign, I confronted the formidable task of selecting individuals to chair the campaign steering committees. In most cases, cochairs were also expected. To recruit forty leadership teams posed a monumental expectation overload. For several weeks, I sat with others trying to discern the gifts necessary for a variety of leadership tasks. We thought. We prayed. We thought some more. Surely, our best choices were already too busy with multiple commitments.

Yet, God continues to provide. I made an initial phone call to each selected person, and followed it with a letter. Two of us met with each individual or couple. We discussed their gifts and their role in the life of the church. We prayed together. Many of them confessed, "I have been looking for a fresh way in which to serve God. This may be my (our) gift."

As they agreed to serve, I rejoiced in my own spirit. A service of dedication was held on a Sunday morning. Within a relatively brief period of time, a major task was accomplished. The congregation celebrated. God had given us guidance.

The leadership yield from that experience lingers. God always confounds human wisdom and expectation when we ask others to receive what God has given!

CHAPTER 4

DISCOVERING EMERGING GIFTS

I recently invited a new member of the congregation to a weekday breakfast meeting. Something intrigued me about his obvious love for the church and his eagerness to become a member. I knew that he had been successful in his business over the years. He might respond positively to a developing capital campaign.

With inward hesitancy but outward boldness I approached the subject with him—suggesting a specific three-year gift. His response astounded me: "Brian, we would be happy to give that gift." Then he added: "For some reason, God has given me the ability to make money. I need some guidance to ensure that I use that blessing wisely." In one self-revelatory moment, he identified his own "gift of giving," one of the most important spiritual gifts mentioned in Scripture.

Throughout his writings, Paul identifies a variety of spiritual gifts. He seldom explains these gifts in any depth. One notable exception is the gift of "love" in 1 Corinthians 13. Early readers already possessed some working knowledge of the place of spiritual gifts in congregational life.

A few of the often mentioned gifts include: wisdom, knowledge, faith, healing, miracles, prophecy, discernment of spirits, speaking in tongues, service, pastoral care, ministry, exhortation, and giving. (See 1 Cor. 12:4-11; Rom. 12:5-8; Eph. 4:11.)

As varied as these gifts seem, they only begin to address the issue. Furthermore, the list of all gifts in the New Testament text is certainly not a complete listing, even for that time. Gifts abounded in the first century, *and are abundant now.* The list of spiritual gifts expands as new arenas for mission emerge. God reveals new ways to build up the body of believers.

The world continues to change. Specific gifts will take on fresh importance during the next few years. These gifts will equip the church for the coming generations. Even now, God is preparing those gifts. Leaders who love and understand the church will continue to identify and call forth their gifts.

Where and how is God making these gifts known? Which gifts are most critical? Which are most abundant? How may they be identified? Who will discern spiritual gifts, ancient and new?

This chapter will explore a few of the emerging gifts. While not necessarily new to the Christian experience, they *are* gifts awaiting new discovery. Their development will require the commitment of the church and its leadership as we move into the next century.

The Gift of Giving

An effective and balanced ministry requires significant financial undergirding. A portion of that undergirding comes from leadership gifts. Biblical leadership recognizes and calls for the gift of giving. Such a call always elicits positive responses. Furthermore, the exercise of the gift of giving creates growing disciples.

Garry works within the financial structures of a major corporation. He is highly trained in his field. He is also a maturing Christian. Garry's faith developed through a combination of factors: regular worship, attentive listening, volunteering in a soup kitchen, encouragement by family members, and the challenge of a covenant discipleship group. He describes himself as an "atheist caught by the church." His member interests gravitated toward matters of stewardship and finance. He listened attentively when I interpreted Christian giving as *an expression of discipleship.*

As a result of the movement of the Spirit in his life, Garry now leads our annual stewardship campaign with insight and theological integrity. God integrated his financial skills with Christian formation. As he recently began to tithe, he also gained an understanding of giving as a spiritual gift.

Financial giving is an outgrowth of discipleship. Giving is a response to the grace of God. A timeless call of Scripture is that of bringing tithes, thank offerings, votive offerings, and other spontaneous offerings to God. A "collection" is *taken*. However, one makes an *offering* to the God of grace and steadfast love.

Some pastors joke that the most sensitive nerve in the human body runs to the right hip pocket. Leadership development stimulates that nerve to a positive sensitivity. Cultivating leadership giving requires an understanding of the many pockets out of which persons can express a giving lifestyle. Current income represents only one possibility. To ignore accumulated resources or bequests (two other "pockets") is to ignore an essential component of discipleship growth.

For the Christian, only one "pocket" is decisive. That pocket is the one out of which one responds to the call to discipleship. Christian leaders provide clear, convincing, contemporary invitations to discipleship. Christian giving—from whatever pocket—is a response to the experience of God in the midst of life. All pockets reside under the same claim and call!

Giving is the responsibility of every faithful follower of Jesus Christ. Jesus teaches about financial matters or material possessions in sixteen of the thirty-eight recorded parables. More than two thousand verses in the Bible relate to money or material possessions. In contrast, "faith" and "prayer" are the subject of approximately five hundred verses each.

Everyone does not have the means to give large sums of money; but everyone is challenged to be a giver. A missionary in one of the poorest sections of Mexico regularly challenged his congregation to give "something" at each worship service. "If you have no money," he would enjoin, "give a button or a pin. Give something as an offering to God."

While giving is every disciple's call, generous giving is the specific call to a few. Some persons are called by God to exercise the gift of bountiful giving. Paul suggests this in one of his "gift lists."

> We have gifts that differ according to the grace given to us: prophecy, in proportion to faith; ministry in ministering; the teacher, in teaching; the exhorter, in exhortation; *the giver, in generosity.* (Rom. 12:6-8; *emphasis mine*)

Paul knew some persons who clearly had the gift of generous giving. Paul identifies and summons that gift.

Later, he writes to Timothy:

As for those who in the present age are rich . . . they are to do good, to be rich in good works, *generous, and ready to share* . . . so that they may take hold of the life that really is life. (1 Timothy 6:17-19; *emphasis mine*)

An assumption prevails that those who have the means for extraordinary giving are isolated cases or textbook illustrations. We may say, "Surely, they are not a part of *our* circle of Christian friends, or members of *our* congregation." Such an assumption is false! Disciples with the gift of giving emerge regularly. They only await God's prompting and a discerning call.

Many clergy are reticent to approach people regarding their giving. Many are apologetic regarding money issues entirely. Some confess their reluctance: "You all know this is not my favorite subject; but it *is* that time of year again." Some demur, "I am a minister, not a fund-raiser." Some worry about comparisons to recent TV incarnations of Elmer Gantry.

One clergy leader evidences distinct embarrassment when the subject of money is raised at church meetings. His is a mission church with major debt and heavy financial responsibilities. When the "monthly shortfall" is discussed by lay leaders, he visibly hangs his head as though ashamed of the subject.

Clergy leaders who adhere to a theology of spiritual gifts are more likely to overcome an embarrassed inherent reticence to talk about money *and* to call those who are gifted in giving. If we truly discern the gifts of others, we will challenge financially gifted persons to act upon their gift. We act with the boldness that inherently emerges from an ecclesiology of spiritual gifts.

Recruitment of church school staff, officers, committee members, and lay pastors seems easier than to challenge persons with the gift of giving. Money is presumed a private area. Even the identification of those with this gift is considered taboo in some circles. Christian baptism presumably excludes *the baptism of the wallet.*

In presentations before clergy groups on giving, I spend considerable time encouraging hesitant pastors. I remain confident that *the spiritual gift of giving is present in every congregation.*

A Personal Journey Toward Awareness

My understanding of the spiritual gift of giving developed slowly. Realization grew from contact with lay members discovering it about themselves. Leaders taught me because they already knew the reality of the gift. Few knew the *language* of spiritual gifts. Yet many know the *experience* of those gifts.

During the closing years in my second congregation, an affluent church member invited me to meet with him. He told me that he planned to give a substantial gift to a capital project the church was undertaking at the time. The gift was sizable—more than I had ever experienced as a single contribution to the church. He offered it without any invitation or urging from me.

He told me that the gift was given for two reasons: first, God had blessed him in some special ways in recent years; second, he had a great love for the work of the church and its impact upon his life.

After describing his own responsiveness to God's call, he counseled me in my role as a pastor. "Begin to learn to *ask* for larger gifts in the course of your ministry," he said. "Do not be afraid to ask. Invite others to respond to giving as a call from God. Men and women are more willing than you know!"

Intuitively wary of this "opportunity," I did not act upon his advice for almost five years. Then, a second time, awareness of "the gift of giving" came from a lay member who was a growing disciple.

I suggested in a sermon that God might be calling some in *that* worshiping congregation on *that* Sunday morning to exercise the gift of giving in their lives. In essence, the possibility was simply laid upon the people for reflection.

The next day, a phone call came into my office from a man in his early forties. I knew him only slightly. He was the busy president of a small company. He invited me to lunch. As we ate, he said, "My wife and I have been talking since your sermon. We feel your message was addressed to us. I do not have a lot of time for meetings or other leadership in the life of the church; but we think we may have the 'gift of giving' of which you spoke."

As a result of his initiative, this couple became the highest contributing household to the general operating budget of the church for the next few years. They also made the largest offering to *two* subsequent capital projects. While I know little of their financial assets, I am convinced that their offerings reflect a substantial leap of faith. God opened a new door for them and a new door for my ministry!

Months later, I cautiously identified three couples whom I deemed *might* have the gift of giving. I asked them to consider a capital gift for a new pipe organ. All three responded positively. One asked, "How much do you think we should give?" My mind raced for an answer. I suggested a number. He said, "We'll do it. But you need to know that you didn't ask me for enough." I was speechless! My presumed boldness had not been bold enough.

Those who have the spiritual gift of giving need to be challenged in their discipleship, just as assuredly as Sunday school teachers, officers, lay pastors or others need to be challenged regarding their gifts. Those who sense God's gentle push toward greater generosity will often hint at the need for direction from clergy overseers. They need spiritual encouragement to take the next step. Pastors must be sensitive to this movement of the Spirit.

Some men and women confidently believe that they have been given the ability to make money. Many such persons want their gifts to be used in the church as surely as those who sing, teach, pray, or preach. They seek help in using the monetary blessings from their labors wisely. Congregations and growing Christians who understand the ecclesiology of spiritual gifts will recognize the importance of cultivating and encouraging this gift. Jealousy or resentment will not surface. The gift of giving needs the same attention as the gift of teaching, the gift of music, or the gift of administration. A perceptive clergy leader can help these persons see that they are being called to exercise a special spiritual gift.

Persons with the gift of giving express it in varied ways. Some are eager to give to missional causes. They understand the outreach ministry of the local church. They feel God's call to support missional projects. They exercise their gift at special times and seasons.

Some persons want to give substantially to human emergency crises. They want to be called when a congregational member is in danger of losing a home or a car. They want to assist with special medical needs, or when someone needs professional counseling. They will remind a pastor/leader to provide them the opportunity to fund these needs.

God not only presents the gift of giving, God also diversifies that gift. *Such is the mystery of all spiritual gifts.*

The responsibility of the spiritual leader is to raise the issue of the gift of giving without apology. The suggestion to consider giving as a spiritual gift should be made several times each year. Such suggestion comes through individual consultation, teaching, preaching, or written articles in the church newsletter. The simple witness of others can be a testimony to the joy of giving.

The summons to the gift of giving will not immediately be heeded by everyone who possesses the gift. Some affluent Christians may want to defer their decision in order to seek the counsel of their financial advisors.[2] Some will laugh politely, and change the subject. But few will consider the suggestion of this gift to be insulting. They are honored to be asked. They value dialogue on the matter at different points in their pilgrimage. They genuinely want guidance in being faithful.

A challenge to the gift of giving is an antidote to the secular gods of consumerism, the leisure industry, and entitlements. The creeping tide of secularization brings a plethora of dangers. Pervasive human emptiness persists as secular gods lure and entice major dollars. These gods of hedonism give false expectations regarding personal fulfillment. The soul of a Christian steward is enriched through the discovery of the gift of giving. *Cheerful, generous Christians always become spiritually vigorous people.*

The Gift of Volunteer Service

Jane is a weekday volunteer at the front desk. She has a cheerful voice and a quick memory for names. She has good instincts regarding appropriate responses for unusual questions. Having relocated around the country many times, she is especially able to make personal connections with visitors and out-of-town callers. Jane is the personification of the term "connectional." She uses a spiritual gift to excellent advantage.

Sociologists suggest that the most critical resistance in the church during the next 15 to 20 years will not be money but time. The increasing pace of life and the proliferation of leisure options compete for our discretionary hours. The number of hours available for leisure has shrunk by 30 percent or more over the past 20 years. Those who volunteer time are shrinking in number. Many nonprofit organizations, including churches, are encountering a rapidly decreasing volunteer base.

In spite of prevailing trends that seem to consume discretionary time, men and women *do have* time to give. Many people are unaware that the church needs their time. They do not realize the myriad of large and small tasks to which they can make a substantial contribution.

Volunteer service comes from a variety of sources: the recently relocated, the retired, empty nesters, mothers with children in school, and persons who volunteer service in other community and civic groups. Leadership through spiritual gifts maintains a careful vigil over volunteer options and those who may volunteer. Some churches enlist a volunteer "volunteer coordinator" to oversee both the options and the spiritual gift.

Telephone receptionist volunteers enable administrative support personnel to use their skills to better advantage with fewer distractions. The church has more accurate documentation and fewer scheduling conflicts when volunteers use these gifts. Different telephone volunteers have differing gifts, and can be used for specific needs. Some are excellent "generalists" at the phone. Others are better at recruitment of coffee hosts. Still others are most effective in calling "lists" of persons to update information.

A group of retired men came together a few years ago for a work day at the church. Finding fellowship and a purposeful outlet for their skills, "The United Methodist Men's Upper Middle Aged Maintenance Management Consortium" was born. For years, they have continued to gather each Tuesday morning. Their efforts in painting, carpentry, electrical work, landscaping, refinishing, and other special areas have saved the church thousands of dollars. They have also found a special meaning for the retirement years.

This "consortium" has also engaged in outreach projects in small, city churches. Such churches may have few able-bodied members to take on even simple tasks. A Christian housing ministry in the metropolitan area benefited from the volunteer gifts of our retired men. Their gift of volunteer service in the life of the church is a demonstration of discipleship.

Expand the base of volunteer gifts. A few suggestions: (1) assembling worship bulletins and major mailings—the gift of busy hands; (2) mailing financial giving statements every few months—knowing the importance of confidentiality; (3) serving in an elderly adult day care center—recognizing the value of "space" for the employed caregivers to have a respite lunch hour; or (4) functioning as a music librarian—working alone in precious quiet to sort, store, and retrieve choir anthems.

Several dozen church newsletters cross my desk each week. Thriving churches seem to be those where imaginative leaders regularly call volunteers in skilled and unskilled areas. A large church in Oklahoma City relocated their entire building about four miles from their former site. The new worship room features many live plants and trees—an expression of God's creation. The pastor issued a call for persons who would care for this array of growing things on a weekly basis. Sixty persons responded. Each volunteer is trained for a task that will consume about two hours each Thursday morning throughout the year.[3] Does your church have some flower or shrubbery beds that might benefit each growing season from several volunteers? Who has the gift of growing things?

One of the groups overlooked for exercising volunteer service is the youth of the church. While many teens are searching for ways to earn money, they also respond to opportunities for volunteer service. As the demands upon their lives become more frenetic, teens need meaningful involvement. The church can become an important laboratory for exploration of God-given gifts. Youth who discover their spiritual gifts early become productive, satisfied, and capable adults. A "volunteer coordinator" can add to this aspect of the total ministry of a church. Such an individual must know the ecclesiology of spiritual gifts, and exhibit that ecclesiology in the position. The task is *always* more than merely filling spaces. Such persons engage in a complex matching of volunteers to service. The "volunteer coordinator" *can be* a paid staff position, but may also be volunteer.

Every vital congregation watches for opportunities to reclaim gifts of volunteer service. Christian leaders who do not see this effort as an expression of ministry endanger the spiritual energy of the church. They also capitulate to powerful secular forces that lure people's discretionary time in nonfulfilling endeavors.

The Gift of Group Leadership

John came to Christ Church with a special affinity for outreach projects. At first, I was reluctant to ask too much of him because of his heavy company responsibilities and travel schedule. However, we needed a chairperson for our Adult Day Care board. We needed a tenacious and compassionate leader who could direct that ministry through a time of real crisis. The ministry itself *and* the feelings of the congregation were at stake.

In response to a spiritual prompting, I arranged an appointment and asked John to serve. He asked when the term of office began. Hesitantly,

I replied, "Right away." After two days of prayerful thought, he agreed. He spent two weeks reading several years worth of meeting minutes. He initiated interviews with present and former board members. He claimed leadership of the board with a vigorous spirit. John has the spiritual gift of leadership.

Paul reminds us of this gift in at least one instance: "And God has appointed in the church . . . forms of assistance, *forms of leadership*" (1 Cor. 12:28; emphasis mine). Elsewhere, Paul suggests that those who have the gift of administering leadership should do so with diligence. (See Rom. 12:8.)

Specific Christian leadership contributes directly to the building up of the body and the work of ministry. (See Eph. 4:12.) The church needs leaders who can influence people toward the attainment of goals. Every church needs the gift of leadership. Not always easy to discern, we succumb to models from the secular and corporate worlds.

A person with the spiritual gift of leadership is not *necessarily* a person who is president of a company or CEO of a large corporation. Nor is it necessarily the person who has time management skills, one who is knowledgeable in "management by objectives," or even "Total Quality Management." Persons with genuine spiritual leadership gifts are persons who have a servant orientation. They care about people. They are well grounded in their own devotional life. They know the nature and purpose of the church. They *may also be* recognized leaders in other arenas of life. However, some of the best leaders in our churches have not attained anything remotely similar to executive status in the world.

Support group ministry is most in need of the gift of leadership. The demand for support groups will be extensive in years to come. Many congregations already have support groups for divorce recovery, grief recovery, for those battling cancer, stroke, or other illness, the unemployed, those who fight bouts with depression, and mothers of young children. Emerging groups in the church now support parents of gay and lesbian children, or work with family members where one individual receives an HIV positive diagnosis. What other groups for support will be needed tomorrow?

Christian support groups differ from those in the culture around us. For example, cancer support groups in hospitals or United Way agencies offer clinical and educational support for cancer patients and their families. Cancer support groups in the church offer a place to listen, to share questions and fears, to laugh, to cry. Members pray for one another. Church based groups also offer a different kind of hope. Christian hope reflects our confidence in the ultimate victory over all disease, whether physically cured or not. The leader of a cancer support group will understand these differences. Members offer listening skills as well as the comfort of Scripture and prayer. God raises up leadership for Christian support groups as the needs arise. Leadership for unemployment support might come from a person who knows something about the dynamics of employment referral agencies, benefits, or résumé preparation. Such a leader would also understand the importance of maintaining self-worth, while surviving day to day without a job.

Leadership for a group of parents of gay and lesbian children might be a couple who have such a child, and who are able to extend a supportive hand to those in a similar situation. While understanding honest differences of opinion about same-sex relationships, leadership for this group in the church maintains a strong commitment to the sacred worth before God of both heterosexual and homosexual persons.

Occasional, Short-Term Leadership

Sometimes a support group need arises quickly, at a critical time. During Operation Desert Storm in the Persian Gulf in 1991, few support groups existed in our area for parents, spouses, and others who had loved ones serving in that area. In the search for support group leaders, we found both a retired army officer and a former air force chaplain in the congregation. Both of them brought Christian leadership to anxious people. In addition, a man who had been separated from his family while in Vietnam shared his insights and offered hope and comfort to the group.

When natural disaster strikes an area, governments and social services emergency units may quickly respond. The church has the gift of spiritual support that others are not equipped to bring. Such support may be needed for many months, even years.

Clergy and other staff may lack time to fill all support group needs. A willingness by some of the laity to respond is vital. Clergy or employed staff may need to *initiate* a group. Certain "start-up" skills and group building exercises are required. But this does not mean that the clergy or staff members must be the anchor that holds the group in place.

A positive response to real needs is at the heart of our calling. Remember: *God provides the gifts necessary to do what God needs us to do through the church in any given situation.* Group leadership is waiting to be identified and called forth for the work of the Kingdom. We pray, we seek, we call, and we offer prayers of gratitude to God for the gifts that are discovered and used.

Training Gifted Leaders

Many churches offer training opportunities for new leaders in their congregations. One model for this kind of training includes techniques and styles of running a meeting. Printed manuals are passed out to appropriate persons. Discussion centers around flowcharts and organization procedures. In some cases, clergy train leaders in parliamentary procedure.

An alternative model will be more productive. Offer training on "the spirituality of leadership." Prepare persons to bring spirituality to their leadership style: use of prayer, a devotional reading, listening to God, singing of hymns, an opportunity to share joys or concerns with the group. Attempts to reformulate leadership training in this fashion over the past five years have brought excellent results and positive response from elected and appointed men, women, and couples.

Leadership often appears from unexpected places or in unexpected ways. However, such leadership is no surprise to God.

Gifts for New Family Constellations

Gifts for ministering to the single adult population are imperative. Initiating a singles ministry in your church provides an opportunity for giving single adults fellowship, in-depth growth, and recovery from broken relationships. The church must take singles ministry seriously. Larger churches need concentrated staff support and recognition of singles issues. During the past eight years, our singles ministry has not only grown dramatically in size, but also lay leadership grew rapidly from within.

A corollary to the singles ministry is the strengthening of intact families. Families today have many configurations.[4] The "traditional family" is becoming a minority reality. The vital congregation gives support to traditional families, single parent families, blended families, and extended families. Each form has representation in every congregation. Who can lead church ministries with families? Who has this gift? God is raising up leaders who can support and encourage intact couples and families.

A generation ago, a prominent U.S. senator remarked that we can discern the values of a society by the way we care for those at the extremes of life—the very old and the very young. The church must be in the forefront of leadership in both arenas.

What of the aging population? The county in which I currently reside has the second largest *percentage* of aging population of any county in the United States. AARP groups are active everywhere. Yet, their contribution is limited. The church can rediscover the gifts from God for building and sustaining a ministry with the growing population of the elderly. We are regularly training and employing persons in a weekday adult day care, a two day per week Alzheimer unit, and a "care for the caregivers" monthly ministry.

Often, an outreach ministry for children is limited only by the space available. Licensed day care, short-term drop-in services, and "before and after school" care, are a few of the opportunities.

Some congregations are currently assessing the viability of child care for parents who must work the second shift of the day (3:00–11:00 P.M.) in order to generate sufficient income. Are we responding to the rapidly changing workplace and the impact from such change upon families? God gives gifts to that end. God will raise up leaders when God's people have a vision.

The Gift of Discipleship

A Sunday school teacher completed a special lesson on discipleship. She used stories, pictures, and songs to make her point. When she finished, several children raised their hands to add comments. The teacher was pleased to see the response.

One little girl was particularly anxious to speak. "We disciple everything at my house," she reported. "We disciple plastic. We disciple bottles. And we disciple newspaper, too. My mother says that discipling will save the earth!"

Great truth resides in those words. For many believers, the greatest spiritual challenge is to discipleship. Jesus' first gracious invitation is to follow him. (See Mark 1:16-20; 2:14.) The most important responsibility of the local church is that of training believers in discipleship. Disciples *must be trained* for each new generation.

Discipleship itself may be a spiritual gift. Not everyone was called by Jesus to be a disciple. That truth remains operative today. Many persons believe. Yet, some believers are called deeper. Some are called to exercise the grace of faithful discipleship.

No congregation will persist for long unless it develops at least one small group emphasis that works in its setting. Many viable models for small group ministry exist today. Creative new models emerge regularly. At Christ Church, the most effective current model for small group ministry is covenant discipleship.[5] Presently, about fifteen such groups are meeting weekly—including two for senior high youth (called "branch groups"). Members receive an invitation to participate in a covenant group at least twice each calendar year.

Covenant groups fulfill the critical need for small group ministry *and* meet one of the greatest needs in the contemporary Christian journey: building disciples for the new century.

The comprehensive purpose of the church is clear: (1) invite people, reach out to the unchurched, the unconvinced; (2) help them relate to God, to find a personal connection with the Holy; (3) train them in discipleship; and (4) and send them forth.

The third component of our mission, discipleship, is an outgrowth of the experience of God's grace. Whereas grace is a *gift*, the maturation of discipleship is a *choice*. As an island in a sea of secularization, the church's opportunity is to make discipleship a worthy choice.

During John Wesley's most energetic phase of ministry, he realized the need for continued progress in personal discipleship. Therefore, Wesley called people together in small classes that met weekly. He designated "leaders" for each class. He trained these persons carefully.

Wesley's class system was instrumental in revitalizing eighteenth-century England. Class meetings began with the classic question, "How is it with your soul this week?" Most contemporary Christians would find such a question awkward. Subsequent questions were a "checkpoint" for a class member's progress in spiritual growth.

Wesley's design and encouragement brought results. Christian men and women facilitated mutual growth from "wherever they were" toward "the next step" on their journey.

The Disciple?

What does a disciple look like? What does it mean to "follow" Jesus today? I enthusiastically advocate David Watson's design.[6] That design contains four components. A disciple seeks to develop his or her obedience to Christ through acts of *(1) worship, (2) devotion, (3) compassion and (4) justice* under the guidance of the Holy Spirit.

Worship includes regular and special occasions of reverent gathering by the people of God. Receiving the sacrament of communion regularly is also included. *Devotion* is the private expression of worship: reading and meditation upon Scripture, prayer, daily practice of the presence of God, financial commitments to God's work, and intercessory prayer. These are the essential elements of inreach.

Compassion includes deeds of love and mercy to family members, friends, and neighbors—planned or spontaneous. *Justice* works to transform systems that perpetuate any condition that deprives persons of their fullest humanity: hunger, homelessness, war, illiteracy, family violence, unemployment, and other forces. These are the essential elements of outreach.

Readers will notice a reprise of the elliptical image here. Each Christian seeks growth where he or she feels it most necessary. Each one engages in a covenant discipline to move from "where they are" to "where God may want them to be."

Growth is necessary in all four areas: worship life, devotional life, deeds of compassion, and works of justice. Christian pilgrims strive for personal growth toward wholeness on their own journey.

Initially, covenant groups were labeled as accountability groups. However, "accountability" *can* become a stumbling block. Persons understandably ask, "Why should I be accountable to a brother or sister for faithful obedience in my daily walk with God?"

Clearly, John Wesley saw the importance of accountability. Discipleship without accountability is like an engine without maintenance. Accountability keeps our lives in tune. Covenant discipleship groups provide accountability at several points: (1) agreeing to meet together for one hour each week, (2) agreeing to a specified covenant which is developed by the group, and (3) agreeing to report on faithfulness to that covenant on a weekly basis. This accountability provides transformation and growth.

I can personally testify to the value of accountability in my own Christian journey. I have been in a covenant group for more than nine years. Members of my covenant group—"watching over me in love"—enable me to lead a more deliberate life in Christ. My decision to be a part of this ministry has been one of the most important personal decisions in my own Christian walk.

Good and remarkable things happen when we are accountable for an agreed upon set of Christian disciplines. Weekly accountability for discipleship provides muscle to the Body of Christ and brings strength to the Christian life.

Serendipitous Emerging Gifts

A woman drove to the airport to pick up her two daughters who were home from college. Traffic was backed up at the terminal. She spotted her daughters standing in front of the doors, but they were a block away and she could not get to them. Finally, she stepped out of her car and hollered as loud as she could, "Alice! Kathy!" They heard her voice and made their way to the car. Whereupon the man sitting in the car behind her said, "Lady, would you mind calling for Harold?"

Sometimes we simply let gifts emerge, and then we rejoice. An individual may discover his or her gift and begin to exercise it without specific direction. Serendipity is a characteristic of the Spirit.

Bob lives in disability retirement as the result of a war injury. He can not walk great distances, so he spends a great deal of time each day in his car. He loves his church.

Ten years ago, he began cruising the boundaries of the church property looking for any broken glass or trash to be picked up. He checked the exterior of the buildings each night looking for open windows or doors.

One Sunday morning, he began parking cars as people arrived. Today, he brings orderliness to the parking. He knows children by name. He knows persons with handicapping conditions, and guides them to the closest available spot. He has the gift of organizing parking, *as well as gift of hospitality.* By the grace of the God who gives many gifts, Bob is now an asset in our parking lot with his orange vest and bright smile. With decreasing physical mobility, Bob is training an "heir apparent" to the task—another in whom the gifts are growing!

LaRue volunteered to answer the phone early on Sunday mornings. She handled incoming phone calls regarding times of services, sickness or other emergencies, and messages to the clergy. Today, she coordinates a regular team of such persons on a rotating schedule. A Sunday morning caller is cheerfully greeted by a trained volunteer to channel information and messages appropriately. The gifts have simply emerged.

A married couple began working one Sunday each month in an inner city soup kitchen as an expression of their own discipleship. Today, they have assumed responsibility for recruiting and assigning persons from the congregation to that soup kitchen one Sunday morning each month. They have involved the adult and youth choirs, covenant discipleship groups, and youth groups. They encourage Saturday evening worship for those serving in the kitchen on a particular Sunday. Their unsolicited gift emerged.

A man with a passion for hunger ministries began recruiting persons to be "gleaners" in the farm fields around Pittsburgh. Two or three Saturdays each fall, he drives a carload to the fields, assists in the harvest, and delivers the produce to the Pittsburgh area food bank. His gift was not recruited. The gift simply emerged.

When our church installed new sound equipment for the sanctuary, we also acquired a sophisticated recording system to produce tapes for shut-ins. Casual operation of the sound board and its many components was no longer possible. A technician was needed to monitor the sound during worship services and record them.

Doug evidenced some learning disability in his childhood. Even as an adult, he relies primarily upon his ears and "hands on" experience to learn. Sound systems hold a fascination for him. We approached him regarding our needs and asked if he would consider working our new sound board and recording our worship services. Within weeks after he began, tape ministry recipients praised that "new voice" introducing each week's service. They also indicated a distinct improvement in overall tape quality.

An ear for sound, a resonant voice, and a knack for technology emerged as spiritual gifts. Those gifts became an asset to our worship services (inreach) and our tape ministry (outreach).

The gifts of God are for the building up of the Body of Christ, and for the work of Christian ministry. The church is involved in a continuous process of rediscovering an endless line of those splendid gifts. Sometimes they come by design and planning. Sometimes they simply emerge. Either way it happens, we say, "Thanks be to God."

CHAPTER 5

STAFFING: BUILDING A TEAM

Cindy came to the Christ Church staff in 1982. We needed to replace the part-time person who coordinated the new member assimilation program. I asked the personnel committee and the staff to suggest a list of possible candidates.

Cindy's name appeared on several lists. I knew that she had some background in developing orientation programs in the banking industry. More important, I knew she had been a conscientious Christian in her recent journey. She possessed that sense of "presence" which would be positive and encouraging to new member prospects and visitors.

We made an appointment at my office. I outlined the purpose for my call as she listened quietly. Without hesitation, she responded: "I have recently had a prompting from God regarding a call to some form of ministry in my life. Perhaps this is an opportunity God wants me to try."

Over the years, Cindy has grown from part-time new member coordinator into a pivotal presence on the staff. Today, she is director of Christian formation and programming. God has given her exceptional skills for the formation of discipleship groups, program growth, and leadership development. She has gifts for responsive listening to other staff. She utilizes gifts for conflict management and resolution. She quietly envisions new ministries. No one could have anticipated how the Spirit would develop her gifts through the years.

The initial promptings that led us to her continue to be confirmed. Her gifts continue to expand. She guides and strengthens my own leadership gifts. While some large congregations use clergy in her role, she is "evidence" that a gifted layperson can be used in ministry by God. Her story is one expression of the joy of staff building through gifts.

Staffing brings an especially fulfilling expression to the ecclesiology of spiritual gifts. Nowhere are the principles more rewarding. Nowhere is the work of the Spirit more stimulating. Building a team through spiritual gifts brings exhilaration to Christian leadership.

This chapter addresses congregations who are multiple-staffed or who are on the threshold of such development. You may be (1) in the preliminary stages of exploration, (2) firmly committed to a current staff model, (3) looking for a new design, or (4) mired in muck and desperate for creative alternatives. Whatever your present status, an ecclesiology of spiritual gifts has fascinating implications.

You may experience some growth in average worship attendance, in a specific area of membership, or in nonmember constituents. You glimpse a new vision which affects both congregational life *and* community influence. You learn of a specific slice of ministry which seems applicable to your situation. Dare to build the employed leadership team on the basis of God-given gifts.

The ecclesiology of spiritual gifts can be utilized with confidence for building or replacing staff. *There need only be some commitment to the principles by a core group of leaders in order to initiate the process.*

Most churches do not need additional clergy as a first consideration for expanded staffing. Laypersons have God-given gifts to work in the areas of program development and administration. This frees the clergy to oversee and lead in areas for which they are trained. On a practical level, cost considerations for part-time lay specialists make such lay staff development more feasible in the small-to-medium sized congregation. Lay specialists exist among the members because God is at work in the Church!

Many models exist for church staffing. Most common is the appointment of additional clergy. Too often, other options never surface. Additional clergy staff is the automatic choice of the church. Closely related is the decision to look for a director of religious education. Since "worship" and "Sunday school" highlight the church's outside sign, we assume that "educational assistance" is the second logical need.

Some churches search for "talent" in the wider community. They "let the word out" to other congregations, advertise in newspapers, or engage in a national search.

My experience with staffing validates an underutilized principle: *most, if not all, staff can rise out of the membership of the congregation.*[1] This approach entails some risks. However, the possibilities make the risks worthwhile. The larger the membership of the congregation, the more applicable the methodology.

Some congregations easily succumb to arguments *against* employing church members. They may remember one bad experience. Wounds have not healed. The pain of needing to "dismiss" a church member persists.

For the majority, however, the notion of looking within the congregation for staff leadership gifts occurs far too seldom. Even where this practice is common, the model is not always known or utilized. Recently, my building maintenance supervisor informed me that he did not hire a certain individual *because he didn't think we wanted to hire a church member.* We need constant consciousness-raising about this God-given model.

Once again, the larger thesis of this book applies: *there are sufficient gifts in every local congregation to do what God is calling that congregation to do at any particular time.* This is the biblical witness and promise. The promise can be trusted. God is able to do "exceeding abundantly" in the church. (See Eph. 3:20, especially KJV.) Within the theology of spiritual gifts, reassurance for staffing the church abounds!

Initial Questions

The best years of staff building at Christ Church began with a series of "home meetings" more than ten years ago. Facilitators at these meetings asked several key questions: What are the strengths of this church? What are some of the unmet needs in our community? Who are the people most in need of ministry? Such questions afford an opportunity to be visionary, to imagine the future.

In such settings, financial and facility issues need not become a stumbling block. Money and space are secondary. They are issues which will be handled separately. We planted a single question in the minds of members before the home meetings: What ministry would we tackle in the next five to ten years if money were no object? A corollary question was implicit: What kind of staffing would be required to keep that ministry on target and growing?

All visioning sessions must be free of debilitating questions about money and mechanics. Otherwise, "*What if . . . ?*" never gets asked, and "*Do you suppose that we might . . . ?*" never gets spoken. Concern for money and building stifles the vision. Lean into the Spirit of God and imagine where God might be leading.

Similar questions may be asked at a day-long leadership retreat. A series of three-hour evening "miniretreats" also provide a workable arena. Lean into the Spirit of God and allow that Spirit to move and work.

Such an approach is not naive. This strategy is a passageway to theological integrity. The methods are a catalyst for bold new ventures. Any time spent envisioning ministries and the requisite staff models is time well spent.

Perhaps your church and community have a growing body of youth who need someone to walk with them in discipleship. They need a mature Christian presence who will relate them to God and give them some moral structure upon which to hang their lives.

Perhaps you see increasing numbers of families with younger children being drawn to your church. Younger families are moving into nearby housing. Such influx brings an acute need for a strong children's ministry, Sunday school, weekday ministry, and quality nursery care.

Dream the impossible dreams. Envision a church orchestra, a community clinic for preventive health care, a food bank, a food service ministry, an alternative worship experience, or a ministry to homeless families. Whatever the idea, assume the potential is available to make it a reality. No idea is too ridiculous or farfetched. No one is allowed to say, "*This may be a foolish suggestion, but . . .*"

What kinds of staffing—even minimal part-time staffing—are necessary to hone the growing edge of your ministry? Whatever issues surface as your priority, the principle remains intact: *most staffing in our churches ought to come from the body of laity within the membership.*

What about costs? Obviously, we cannot be reckless. When a church dreams aloud, and when God is trusted for those dreams, miracles happen. Frequently, "seed money" becomes available from a member with the gift of giving.[2] A congregation that believes its dreams are of God will not be afraid to ask. If God is trusted in the process, God is faithful to provide. The position can be fully funded once the image is visible and integral to the ministry of the congregation.

As my second church appointment grew in size, the management of financial resources expanded beyond the capacities of a volunteer. A recently retired member of the congregation sensed the dilemma. He also knew that salary options were essentially prohibitive. He made an offer we could not refuse. "I will manage the finances for two years," he said.

"You pay me a monthly stipend according to the value of the work. I will return at least 90 percent of it to the church—after satisfying any personal income tax liabilities." His presence in this fashion gave us (1) much needed financial oversight, (2) an economically feasible solution, and (3) time to prepare the church for a part-time salaried position within two years. His gifts brought the church far more than we knew.

Implementation Begins

Once the needs for ministry are identified and prioritized, the church employs lay specialists to assist in its ministry. Many times, such employment means only a modest financial stipend. A predominantly lay team—with the right spiritual gifts—facilitates remarkable vitality in a congregation. Growth, undergirded by good planning, will be guided by God's Spirit.

A few years ago, I was preparing a presentation on staffing issues for a group of newly appointed senior ministers. I asked one of our lay staff associates what advice I should give. She replied immediately: "Tell them to hire a few bright, pushy women, and then get out of the way!" More truth exists in this advice than I first realized. Find the *right persons* with the *right gifts* from among the church members, and then *let God use them mightily!*

It takes energy and patience to develop staffing based on spiritual gifts. The larger the church, the longer the process may take. A spiritually healthy model for staffing does not happen overnight. Patience becomes an important virtue.

When highway planners design a new major roadway, they know the importance of site preparation and reinforcement. Without such preparation, the highway will not endure heavy traffic.

Staff selection according to spiritual gifts is the durable foundation for the church's journey. Careful planning and design are crucial. Careful procedures ensure a stable, resilient, long-term ministry. They also bring vocational joy for the long haul.

What About Qualifications?

The selection of a lay staff on the basis of spiritual gifts does not preclude the need for some basic skills. Spiritual gifts are usually discovered as an outgrowth of certain talents or educational training. Seldom do the God-given "charismata" simply "show up" out of nowhere!

Peggy was in her midthirties. She had been a member of the church for several years. She possessed a deep personal faith and a strong background in education. She had worked for twelve years in an alternative high school setting. She taught youth who had difficulty with adjustment in the public schools.

Peggy was invited to consider a youth ministry position at a point when her own daughters were reaching their teenage years. She sensed a need to move beyond her present work. She was experiencing a call to use her training in an area of Christian ministry. In our initial conversation, she quipped, "Who else do you know that *wants* to do full-time youth work?"

She began in part-time status as youth director and children's ministry coordinator. A special monetary gift by a member raised her position to full-time within six months. She studied to become a diaconal minister while working with the youth and their families in the church. Eventually, youth ministry became her full-time vocation. Her gifts for ministry with youth grow exponentially over the years.

Carol began as a part-time financial secretary more than a decade ago. She had considerable training and experience with computers. Working with various church financial campaigns, she also developed numerous mentoring relationships with a variety of stewardship consultants. She familiarized herself with resources and attended workshops. She gained confidence in the sensitive area of stewardship formation. Responding to her emerging gifts, the church created a new position for her as director of stewardship and computer services. Today, her spiritual gifts are virtually indispensable.

People broaden their capabilities when they are encouraged to use skills or training. Spiritual gifts bloom within the community of believers. Too often, such vocational experiences are absent in the corporate world. In the church, persons find freedom to develop their gifts—perhaps even creating a new ministry position—rather than conform to externally imposed structures.

Occasionally, emerging gifts have little to do with specific training or educational background. Sue is the resourceful mother of three. She is also an extraordinarily effective coordinator of children's ministries. While her educational background is in teaching science, her personal affinity in the church was children's Sunday school. We invited her to try a part-time position in children's ministry even though it had no discernible relationship to her formal training. God awakened gifts in her that we could not have imagined. Her energy for creative new ideas is astounding.

As we were unable to hold our vacation Bible school during the day because of a major building program, Sue developed a model for the evening hours. Using new images and a different time of day, children and staff experienced an exciting adventure at the church. Sue also brainstormed our "Until School Starts" ministry during a public school strike.[3] This creative response to a community crisis received newspaper and television publicity. The entire community rejoiced in her resourcefulness.

We eventually sought to expand Sue's position to fulltime. The success of her efforts and the growing numbers of young children make such expansion imperative.

Read and review résumés? Yes! But know that God can use persons whose most authentic résumé lies deep within.

Staffing through the use of spiritual gifts has additional advantages. Church member staff know the joys and concerns of the church from the inside. They bring an extra measure of commitment. This is *their* church. They experience aspects of congregational life which reach beyond their specific employee concerns. They know names and mingle with members at informal or festive events. Church member staff are not on the outside, guiding; they are on the inside with a personal stake in the future.

Lay staffing also ensures that the church belongs to the people. When the senior minister changes, the work continues, because member staff remain. The strength of the church is not built solely around the strengths of the senior clergy. Staffing through spiritual gifts is synergistic.

Staff Selection Issues

Sensitive issues arise in hiring church members. Certain standards are important in the selection procedure. Each time a final selection is made, the senior minister should hold a concluding interview with the individual. The individual must understand that the position will be on a trial basis initially. A three month, six month, and one year review mechanism is outlined. At any stage of that review calendar, the church or the employee can determine that the situation is not working as well as expected.

As a matter of pastoral and supervisory concern, I always make the following brief statement to every potential staff/church member: "You will be working with me as both a church member and an employee. There may come a time when I must exercise a supervisory responsibility which seems to negate our pastoral ties. Such a development *could* happen at some point along the way. Do you understand that possibility?"

Even when great care is taken—with prayer, good interviews, and consultation with others—the human component inherent in this procedure can fail us. God gives the gifts and we are led by God's Spirit. But mistakes in judgment can occur. Not everyone can adapt their skills to the special environment of the church. Attitudes in the church differ from those in the secular workplace. A certain woman phoned her banker to arrange for the disposal of a $1,000 bond. The voice on the phone asked her for clarification: "Is the bond for conversion or redemption?" The confused woman paused for a moment, and then asked, "Am I talking to the bank or the church?" Unless a person understands something of the ecclesiology of the church, he or she may not fit into staff structure. Years ago, we joked with a new building supervisor who worked in the steel mills. We told him he would now have to learn the name "Jesus Christ" in a new context. He did, and served exceptionally well for many years.

Working in a church environment requires special sensitivities. In the church, feelings and personal needs matter. Volunteer teams, unrelenting demands, and numerous hurting people come through the doors every day. The summons to sensitivity, compassion, love, and understanding cannot always be answered. Not everyone is able to go the extra mile. Not everyone can overlook or forgive the persistent idiosyncrasies of certain church members.

Furthermore, some persons with excellent programmatic, administrative, or secretarial skills may not be able to cope with church procedures. Others may be unable to handle all the components of a hectic church calendar. Some may not have the capacity to work with volunteer groups. Those with the technical skills and strong references may not have the necessary human relations skills.

Growing Within the Staff Position

The serendipity factor in the ecclesiology of spiritual gifts is astounding! Growth will confirm the call. Frequently, greater skills will open in a related area of ministry.

Judy has been senior administrative assistant during most of my tenure at Christ Church. Her volunteer gifts in music are well attested. She has perfect pitch and a compelling solo voice. Her vocational desire has always been in some area of music. In spite of severely limited time and finances, she initiated courses of study in church music during summer sessions. She was certified as a music associate in The United Methodist Church. We found a way to combine her existing staff position and leadership of a children's choir within budget parameters. Her church strives to help her realize her dreams and use her gifts as a member of the staff configuration.

John came to Christ Church as organist ten years ago. His proficiency as a "service musician" is a true gift. However, existing resources allowed us only part-time funding of the position. John needed full-time employment. As his competency at the organ became apparent, ways were sought to expand his gifts. After considerable planning, I asked him to add "director of worship life" to his position description. The gift for designing and writing worship services quickly became apparent. Today, John continues at the organ console with extraordinary mastery. He also writes all worship services, coordinates volunteer worship personnel (altar guild, ushers, communion stewards), and oversees other worship-related matters. He is "organist" *and* "director of worship life." His gifts have matured abundantly.

A Word of Caution

A sign on a narrow road starting an ascent in the Rocky Mountain National Park reads, "Never overestimate the width of this road." The same principle holds true for staffing. All decisions to build a lay staff, add new staff, or reconfigure a staff model ought to be processed through the appropriate administrative channels. The senior minister is the principal overseer. He or she exercises the option for a final selection. Nevertheless, decisions regarding staffing should not be made without consultation. A decision to create a new staff position or to fill a vacant position ought to be reviewed by appropriate committees. A final recommendation comes from the senior minister—the overseer of gifts—after appropriate interviews.

Clergy leaders articulate the vision along the way. But there must be careful spade work so that the seeds of that vision can thrive and mature. Deviation from this process can cause dissention, and can impede further growth for extended periods of time. Using correct procedure provides a sense of ownership. Proper procedures also provide regular teaching opportunity. A well led design can be used to educate, inform, inspire, and motivate persons regarding the nature of the church and its leadership.

Monitoring the Lay Staffing Style

A seminary student once wrote, "Life is like a chicken trying to lay an egg on an escalator. As soon as you get settled in, the bottom moves out from under you." Most church staffing is a shifting continuum. Life changes, congregational moves, and altered attitudes can affect the process dramatically. Continued support and encouragement from the leader is essential.

Having a strong member staff model in place does not automatically imply that mainstream church members will own and support the model. Support can be especially problematic when finances become tighter than they usually are.

A major vehicle for sustaining congregational support is preaching. Tell the stories of staff building. Worshipers need to know that their church is led by persons who are called into specific forms of employment. The function of the congregation is to be faithful stewards of the mysteries of God. (See 1 Cor. 4:1.)

Teaching is a second vehicle, especially with newer members. New member orientation sessions provide an important opportunity to introduce the theology of spiritual gifts. Point out part-time and full-time staffing from the congregation. When new members meet the staff who were "once as they are," they see God's possibilities at work in others. They can imagine similar possibilities in their own journey. Significant internal dialogue can occur as they hear and assimilate the stories of another's faith journey. At least five times each year, new member classes hear the Christ Church story about staffing (and leadership development) through spiritual gifts from me.

Current staff members ought to have the freedom to suggest refinements of existing staff models. Clergy leaders need to trust lay staff insights in this area without relinquishing the "overseer" responsibility. Any altered or expanded staff design should include input from key program people as well as administrative and support staff.

Employed staff members reflect upon their own gifts *and* become aware of new expressions of what God bestows. Such persons thereby expand their understanding of spiritual gifts. Repeated reminders enhance the total ministry of the church.

Sometimes God is growing something right before our eyes, and we are too preoccupied to notice. Fresh discovery is an integral part of the active pursuit of an ecclesiology of spiritual gifts.

Position Descriptions

Many churches—especially larger ones—use complex instruments for the "review" of employed staff. Numerous hours are spent in attempts to write, perfect, and appropriately utilize these instruments. I consumed inordinate amounts of time in such pursuits during the first three years of my present appointment. In part, this effort was sustained by the steady encouragement of my corporate-type advisory committee. My files are full of futile forms—attempts at perfection and redesign. None of them felt appropriate to the gospel or to the church.

I have been called by colleagues from across the country asking for written information on how we exercise staff performance reviews in my church. Some of these clergy leaders have experienced repeated frustration in this arena of their leadership. They want to know my system. In most cases, I give a simple answer. We review and grow staff utilizing "position descriptions." A few clergy are disappointed in this response. They seem to *want* more structure to the strategy.

Position descriptions are a tool for staff development. Like the multiple options on a quality audio system, position descriptions offer opportunity for fine tuning spiritual gifts. Each employed person on a church staff must have a position description. Position descriptions are written to reflect *both* the tasks to be done *and* the specific strengths inherent in the employee.

No position description ought to continue for longer than one year without review. Generally, a fixed position description is not refined until six months after one begins employment. Each staff member should meet with the senior minister (or another designated supervisor) at least once each year to review the position description. Any appropriate changes are made at these annual sessions. Sometimes, the changes are merely for clarification. Sometimes they are substantial. This annual consultation includes discussion as to whether or not the staff member believes the description fits his or her calling. Most position descriptions undergo some change every year.[4]

The annual review and reassessment reflects a theology of spiritual gifts at work. I prefer the term "developmental review." Such a process is far different from the feared "performance review" in some corporations. The developmental review is a time for appropriate questions in a caring way: How do you feel about your work? How do you sense God's call in this position? How do you feel about your relationship with those who work with you? Are you/we making the best use of your time and gifts in this job? Are there growing edges of this position for you right now? If you could write a new position description for your place on this staff in three to five years, what would it look like? How might the senior minister do a better job in support or advocacy for you?

Annual reviews assist in living out the theology of staffing through spiritual gifts. But faithful oversight is a pulsating continuum. Dialogue takes place with most staff members throughout the year. In regular dialogue, we keep our fingers on that pulse. The practice keeps everyone fine tuning their gifts and leaning into God's spiritual intent for those gifts.

Staff Retreats

Further enhancement of spiritual gifts comes through staff retreats. Busy schedules and family commitments often make 100 percent participation on such retreats difficult. Yet, meeting together two or three times each year for nurture, revisioning, and support is vital.

I provide two one-day retreats *and* one multiple-day retreat each calendar year. The day-long retreats offer time for spiritual renewal and reflection on a single issue. The agenda for at least one of the retreats is the state of the spiritual gifts of staff members. What gifts do they see operative? What emerging needs are on the horizon? How can the full team assist any one member of the team in better expression of his or her gift? Occasionally, the staff participates in "gift bombardment" as part of closing worship (described in chapter 3).

Longer retreats (usually noon to noon over three calendar days) offer a rich opportunity for study of a devotional classic or planning a new dimension to the church's ministry. Such events occasionally utilize an outside resource person. Longer retreats allow for recreation. They provide opportunities for extended conversations in informal settings. They can be a minivacation. Living together enables the staff to become more unified.

A prudent leader will build the cost of such retreats into the church budget. As an alternative, seek a special financial gift to this end each year.

Correction and Accountability

Each member of the staff is assigned a liaison person from the church's personnel committee.[5] Meetings for dialogue are encouraged at least twice each year. The liaison is an additional source of support and clarification of the position description. Their function is to become the congregational representative for the staff person. Matters needing attention are then reviewed with the senior minister and the personnel committee.

What about corrective advice by the overseer? Some confrontation is necessary from time to time. Disagreements regarding procedure, policy, and priorities do occur. Christian leadership and basic courtesy dictate that such occurrences should never happen in public or in front of other staff members. To use staff meetings to correct or criticize a team member erodes the support and confidence of the team. I have observed such occurrences, and they are counterproductive. Even when the authority is clear, exercise of that authority in public settings is badly misplaced.

Occasionally, it is appropriate for additional persons (a member of the personnel committee or a trusted colleague) to be present during discussion or disagreement. These sessions should take place behind closed doors and in the spirit of Christian concern for the individual. A servant leader tries to remain consistently temperate, whether in instances of disagreement or open insubordination. Such restrained behavior is difficult at times. Human emotions easily take charge, and can rush out of control. However, one always advises and confronts an individual in ways that are an expression of grace.

Occasionally, it is necessary to terminate a staff member. Termination can be awkward when the individual is a church member. Nevertheless, such action is necessary from time to time for the health of the church and the health of the staff team.[6] Dismissal can usually be handled jointly by senior clergy and the chair or representative of the personnel committee. Dismissal is subsequently reported to others with care and respect for the person as a child of God. Dismissal also recognizes—publicly and privately—the possibility of other gifts and graces which might be employed elsewhere.

In at least three instances, full-time member staff terminated their membership when dismissed from a staff position at Christ Church. None of these situations were easy. However, neither did they cause me to doubt or rethink the issue of spiritual gifts of members for staffing positions. *The ecclesiology of spiritual gifts is worth the occasional risk and struggle.*

A lay staff position may occasionally expand beyond the person's ability to be effective. One congregation found it necessary to "relocate" a staff member to another position. What she initially provided in a small missional setting was inadequate in a more sophisticated large church setting. She was not able to grow as the job expanded. Her position had simply outgrown her skills. The energy drain by the church on her behalf was considerable. Leaders worked hard to discover her other gifts and reallocate them.

In such situations, the church must continue to trust God for guidance. We are not exempt from staffing problems simply because we are a church! However, we deal with staffing issues differently than does the corporate world. Like the disciples in the boat, the church can survive the staff storm. (See Mark 4:37-41.) Be ready to address necessary changes when the need arises.

Spiritual Gifts of the Associate Clergy

An advocacy position regarding lay staffing in the church does not ignore the ordained clergy. Clergy need to be appointed or called according to their gifts as well. While primarily called to the exercise of word, sacrament, and order, the clergy have other gifts to utilize.

In most situations, a senior clergy person of a congregation is called, assigned, or appointed according to his or her gifts.[7] Ideally, these gifts correspond with the direction and vision of the congregation. Matching clergy with a congregation requires intense effort, but it is time well spent. In at least one denominational polities, the choice unfolds according to precise guidelines. A mission statement is written by the church. Clergy are then interviewed and called according to ways in which their gifts match the mission statement.

In the appointive system, a bishop and cabinet of superintendents match the known conditions of a congregation with the gifts of clergy. This is the normative procedure when *one* ordained clergy is appointed to *one* local congregation. Human conditions and individual family needs may make this approach difficult in some situations. Also, procedures on paper do not always operate as expected in the field.

When *more than one clergy* serve a single congregation, the mechanics require special care. However, the theology and practice of the principles of spiritual gifts apply. Within an ecclesiology of spiritual gifts, the ordained associate is not automatically the "youth person" on staff. Nor is the associate appointed only to visit the shut-ins, recruit teachers for the Sunday school, and provide leadership of the floundering men's group. The day when the "job" of the associate was to do whatever the senior minister chose *not* to do is over! A new set of guidelines applies.

One thesis of this book is the unwitting relinquishment of lay ministry to the clergy. A corresponding point needs to be made. To habitually place associate clergy in positions of youth ministry, music ministry, program development, newsletter production, or other areas often perpetuates inadequate use of their spiritual gifts.

Once lay staff are well placed, the position descriptions for associate clergy require careful deliberation. Most congregations discover that associate clergy have minimal enthusiasm for a position that simply "assists" the senior minister. They take no special joy in only doing what the senior minister cannot do or chooses not to do. The associate clergy need a position description that reflects (1) a growing edge of the church's ministry, (2) expectations around his or her own spiritual gifts, and (3) opportunity and encouragement for personal growth.

Assume a time when the position of associate clergy opens on a church staff. The *first priority* of the staff-pastor relations committee is to write a position description that reflects the areas in the life of the church needing the greatest attention from ordained persons.

Suppose the focus is upon *congregational care.* The position description calls for an individual who can manage people well, who can train and equip lay pastors, who can develop systems for comprehensive care giving, and who exemplifies good pastoral care. While other minor issues may be written into the proposed position description, the administration of care is primary.[8] An associate minister for congregational care might not be *doing* the care so much as *overseeing others* giving the caring.

Another possibility might be a singles ministry. As already indicated, a strong singles ministry is vital to the church. A clergy associate for singles addresses issues of young adults, the widowed, the separated and divorced, and the never married. Sessions for divorce recovery and grief work necessitate specific programming. The clergy staff person for singles must view singleness as a valid option for living, not a "condition" to be "healed." Singles need attention and creative programming in the changing demographics of our society. Churches that reach the breadth of a community will take ministry to singles seriously.

A clergy option now emerging is with the "seeker initiative"—a ministry with (mostly) young adults who (a) have little or no church background and (b) who are beginning to discern some spiritual longings in their own lives. Associate clergy who might address this growing segment of the population are beginning to surface. Typically, they are under forty-five years of age and have some special appreciation for the music with which the "seeker" population grew up.[9]

Other options for associate clergy positions might be small group formation, older adult ministry, or community outreach ministries. In the midst of any of these options, confirmation training or a strong Bible teaching ministry might be included. As with the lay staff, the clergy position description is reviewed and refined periodically. The practice of a "developmental review" applies as well.

After writing a position description for associate clergy, the document is delivered to the judicatory body responsible for placement or selection. Request for associate clergy will be initiated on this basis. While this approach often makes clergy "assignment" more difficult, it is the only appropriate way to proceed. A church needs to express the ecclesiology clearly: they will only consider persons in light of the position description. When *specific* gifts and graces are needed, don't abandon hope. Maintain confidence that the process will work. The right person(s) will be found. God has a vision for the church. God will provide clergy leadership to realize that vision.

I can attest to the fruits of such practice. Rightly called and appointed associate clergy give of their strengths to the total ministry. They develop their God-given gifts. They make an enormous contribution to the larger ministry of the church. When considered merely as adjunct to the senior minister, the associate aimlessly flounders. When given a specific and core ministry to conduct, the associate flourishes.

A strong sentiment is emerging for more fully developed gifts in associate clergy, for *career* associates. The church has used associate positions on multiple staffs as a "training ground" where young clergy gain experience and maturity. Once they have sufficient seasoning, they move on to the full responsibility of their own church. Such procedure misuses God-given gifts. Some clergy are eminently suited to long careers as staff associates. I heartily endorse the cultivation of career associates in denominational polity. I believe it will strengthen the church.

Extended Ministries of the Church

Special consideration needs to be given to extended ministries of a local congregation. These are ministries of outreach and service that relate to the congregation, but are primarily a service to the community. Examples include child care centers, adult day care centers, homeless shelters, feeding centers, multifaceted singles ministries, and others. Where does leadership through spiritual gifts fit into the church's outreach?

Answers depend upon the relationship of the ministry to the local church. Is it an extended outreach ministry of the congregation? Or, is it a service to the community through rented space (for example, AA groups, weight loss groups, hotlines for counseling, shelters for abused women and children)? What message does the church want to give to the community through these ministries? What will those who cross the threshold of the church door learn of the church's mission and purpose?

Most outreach ministries housed in the church building are best operated *as an extension of the congregation's life*. Congregational policy needs to define church facilities as designated spaces for ministry and mission. Sacred spaces are not simply "available" for rent by community groups. True outreach ministries are responsive to human need and enhance the quality of life in the community. A statement of purpose for each missional entity explains the program as it fits into the ministry of the congregation.

Leadership in this outreach can easily come from within the membership. The outreach ministry is an integral part of congregational life. Thus, it is quite natural that a member of the church direct the ministry. Ownership of the program placed within the congregation becomes evident to the community at large.

In the changing leadership of the three outreach ministries of our congregation (children, older adults, singles), we have found *member* leadership in seven of eight changes. One additional member provided critical skills for interim leadership in the child care center over several difficult months. Her superb gifts allowed us to take sufficient time to find a permanent replacement.

When the program director is not from the church family, an existing staff member becomes the liaison. This staff member helps the director assimilate into the total ministry of the church. This plan assures that the outreach program continues to project the nature and mission of the church.

Marie was selected as the new director of our growing child care center.[10] She is not a member of the congregation, but has active ties with a neighboring church of another denomination. She welcomed orientation to our expression of outreach, and became an articulate spokesperson for that outreach to hundreds of parents and families.

Marie is an integral part of the staff team. She meets regularly with the staff, participates in workshops on the spirituality of leadership, and shares in staff retreat experiences. She reflects the thrust of our ministry, even though she does not hold membership in the congregation.

Mary Ann, in contrast, is the third "member" director of our Adult Day Care. Her membership ties provide strong, positive public relations skills. She served as an administrative assistant to the previous director. When the executive position opened, Mary Ann was the unanimous choice of the board. Her leadership style is well-suited to the position. She makes a positive contribution to the outreach ministry, to the staff, and to the whole church.

Sometimes a dilemma occurs in selecting volunteer advisory boards for extended outreach ministries. Certain board members are invited to serve because of expertise in accounting, legal matters, or medical skills—common needs in almost every nonprofit board of directors. These persons are not necessarily church members. As such, they cannot be expected to understand the importance of "seeing" the ministry through the eyes of Christian outreach. Selection of board members should be made within this realization. A ratio of three church members to one community-at-large member is advisable.

Strength in Diversity

A rich diversity is the strength of a Christian staff team. Staff members must express a common love for God and enthusiasm for the ministry of the local congregation. An appreciation for the theology of spiritual gifts is essential. However, *diversity is strength* in any church staff, be it large or small, full-time or part-time.

Several tools exist for exploration of staff diversity. One tool relates to birth order in an individual's family of origin. Staff members relate to others with whom they work much as they related within their family of origin. Most senior ministers are first-born children. Many other leadership oriented persons are first-born as well. Two first-born children working together have *some* propensity for conflict. Such conflict is not the fault of either individual. The possibilities are simply present. First-borns have a natural tendency to take charge. Conflict stems from an innate desire for authority. Understanding birth order helps the staff understand why they relate as they do. A healthier interaction develops.

I always ask a prospective staff member about the family of origin and birth order. It enables me to see how they fit into the staff constellation. Diversity in birth order is important. The work cannot be accomplished when everyone wants to be chief of everything.

Another tool for building strength in diversity is the Myers-Briggs Type Indicator (MBTI). This profile gives each person an identity according to basic personality styles. As personal profiles are completed, staff members find their position in each category.[11]

The most beneficial way to use the MBTI is to allow each member of the staff team to complete and score the test. Then share the results of the individual profile. Trained interpretation of the results is most helpful. Most MBTI experts suggest that a healthy staff have at least one person in each of four major category groups. To have too many people in one category means that some aspects of ministry may be weakened. A diversity of profiles will create a more effective staff team.

Roy Oswald, senior consultant with the Alban Institute, recently made some important comments regarding diversity in an interview. He was asked how he would describe the ideal multiple staff. He responded:

> One that has diversity. The more heterogeneous the multiple staff, the more capability they have to reach out and serve a heterogeneous congregation and community. [But] the more diverse your multiple staff is, the harder it is for members of the staff to get along.
>
> [We] almost need a mixture of some similarities and some differences. There needs to be enough similarity so that they have some bridges to cross and so that they are able to stay with each other and like each other. There should also be a sense of collegiality; diversity is honored. . . . If jealousy and envy go on, multiple staff ministry doesn't work.
>
> The ideal multiple staff is marked by diversity and then respect for that diversity. Then, constancy of commitment to work through the differences.[12]

The key to positive strength in diversity lies in the role of the leader. In the exercise of a servant style of leadership, the leader supports the gifts and serves the needs of the staff. Nurturing a diverse staff is a major requirement of the clergy leadership style. This personal leadership style and the gifts of the leader are the theme of the final chapter.

CHAPTER 6

KNOWING SELF:
GIFTS OF THE LEADER

As a child, my favorite radio show was *The Lone Ranger*. Each Monday, Wednesday, and Friday night, I faithfully tuned in to the ongoing saga of the champion of justice. His story has become a symbol for the way many of us fulfill our ministry. We are "lone rangers" doing an assortment of tasks—perhaps only occasionally needing the assistance of a faithful sidekick. The challenges before the church necessitate a new way. The lone ranger is neither adequate nor appropriate.

Paul writes to Timothy, "I remind you to rekindle the gift of God that is within you through the laying on of my hands" (2 Tim. 1:6). Each baptized Christian receives gifts from God. Similarly, each ordained clergy acknowledges and receives one or more spiritual gifts for the ministry of the church at large. Those gifts come as part of the call, at ordination, or through vocational obedience. The assurance is this: called servants of God receive gifts by the work of the Holy Spirit.

One of the overlooked issues in the ecclesiology of spiritual gifts is the gifts of the congregational leader. This omission stunts the growth of ministry. Clergy become so preoccupied with setting plans in motion, so focused upon membership and staff issues that they neglect their own spiritual formation. They become so intent upon fulfilling ministry as clergy generalists that they neglect the cultivation of their own specific gifts.

A parable is often told of a very dignified pastor who was visiting a woman who was sitting in a wheelchair at a nursing home. As the visit closed, the pastor stood to leave. He gently took her hand and prayed a simple prayer, asking God to be with her, to bring her comfort, strength, and healing.

When he finished the prayer, the woman's face began to glow. She said softly, "Pastor, would you help me to my feet?" Not knowing what else to do, he helped her up. At first, she took a few uncertain steps. Then she began to jump up and down. Then she began to dance and shout. She cried with such happiness that the entire nursing home was aroused.

The pastor hurried, red-faced, out to his car. He closed the car door, grabbed hold of the steering wheel, looked up to heaven, and said, "Lord, don't you *ever* do that to me again!"

This prototypical pastor has neglected his apparent spiritual gifts. Before engaging in a personal spiritual gift inventory, however, it is essential to identify appropriate images for Christian leadership that match the theology of divine gifts. These assumptions create a framework within which to discover and cultivate the God-given gifts of the leader.

A Christian Leadership Style?

The question may legitimately be asked: Is there a "Christian" leadership style for the church? I submit that such a style emerges when juxtaposed along side more secular or corporate styles of leadership.

Christian leadership is not authoritarian. The hierarchically structured, dictatorial style of administration is rapidly diminishing in any enlightened organization. While some executives still utilize this method, the style is not keeping pace with current trends in the workplace.

Twenty years ago, executive leaders used the authoritarian/subordination style most successfully. They made no apology for its place in corporate America. The methodology had been effective over many decades.

The authoritarian style remains operative in some churches. A number of clergy maintain personal theological commitment to authoritarian patterns. In a few instances, persistent use of the style is complicated by other factors. Clergy may fear that members are more intellectually astute or more highly educated. Some clergy are hesitant to nominate or appoint effective lay leadership for fear that their own inadequacies may show. Such fears precipitate a more legalistic style of oversight. The same authoritarian stance expresses itself in a heavy, rigid preaching style.

Regardless of the root motivations, recent sociological changes have seen the structure of authoritarian leadership crumbling. Some corporate leaders have opted for early retirement rather than adjust to new leadership models. The emotional energy required to change leadership styles after so many years in that paradigm is simply too draining.

Sometimes, traditional hierarchical leadership evolves into unproductive patronizing. A strong need to be a "father" to the team directs many actions of the leader. The clergy leader claims to be "right" precisely because he or she *is* the leader. This particular style is more present than we may realize. The "lone ranger" continues to ride through the church! The style may stem from the patriarchal images of Scripture, or even from a "messiah" complex. Nevertheless, unintended paternalism can unwittingly immobilize the church. Autocratic forms of leadership are no longer working in corporate systems. They have never been a part of God's vision for the church.

Even a gentler, more enlightened hierarchical style seems unsuitable for development of spiritual gifts among the people of God. Some leaders in the secular arena have spent a fair amount of energy trying to reformulate the hierarchical pyramid so that it will continue to function. They soften previous methods with presumed enlightened sensitivity. A few revisionists have simply modified or flattened the pyramidic structure. The revised model suggests that employees and supervisors are on a more "equal" footing.

Most analysts find this reforming process unsatisfying. Furthermore, a simple shift in the hierarchical pyramid is inadequate to carry the church into a new day.

A simple "hang loose" style of leadership is similarly unproductive. This style may presume some biblical foundation. Paul suggests that we are "neither slave nor free . . . for [we] are all one in Christ Jesus" (see Gal. 3:28, RSV). However, a freewheeling model of leadership frequently represents an abdication of authority altogether. God is not well served when everyone on the "team" simply does his or her own thing without accountability to a plan, a vision, or a visionary overseer.

Coordinating schedules, avoiding unnecessary duplication, and being good stewards of our spiritual gifts requires teamwork and accountability. While Jesus suggested that disciples ought "not let your left hand know what your right hand is doing" (Matt. 6:3), the consequence of a "hang loose" management style in the church can lead to chaos.

A purely collegial style of supervision and control is not sufficient for the church. Those who propose absolute collegiality—meaning autonomy to pursue your own interests—are too idealistic about the sources of accountability for the organization that permits their freedom. All of us need to be accountable. We may be accountable under the banner of grace; but *we are accountable.*

A Christian Leadership Model

The late Robert Greenleaf uses a term which gives shape to Christian leadership. He refers to the effective leader as one who is "first among equals." For the church, this means that each member of the team is a child of God on equal footing with all other team members. However, one individual is the leader—*the first among equals.* The leader is not invested with final authority nor the absolute power of a veto. Rather, the leader is one who guides persons toward a common goal. Greenleaf writes:

> The key question is how power and authority are handled [in the church].
> . . . The major conclusion I have reached after much searching is that we have at long last come to grips with the liabilities in the obsolete idea of the single chief atop a pyramidal structure, and that henceforth the ultimate authority should be placed in a balanced team of equals under the leadership of a true servant who serves as a "primus inter pares," first among equals.[1]

The leader offers encouragement along the way, and affirms the role of each coworker as to his or her particular piece of the vision. The leader arranges for accountability to the agreed upon vision from time to time. Several images may help to illustrate.

as suggested by Robert Greenleaf

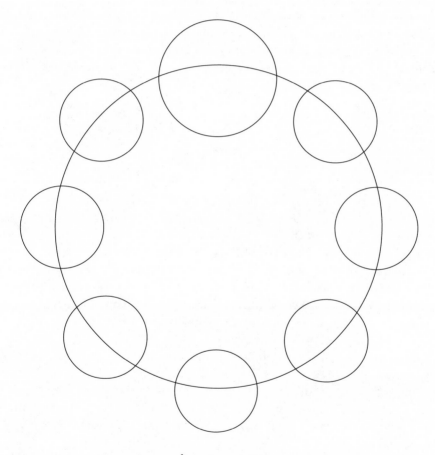

an alternate suggestion

In the language of secular leadership, this is a collegial style with a pyramidic overlay. The leader provides vision and encouragement, but does not pontificate or rule.

Greenleaf uses the term "servant-leader" to describe the ideal "boss" within this paradigm. Using my New Testament ecclesiology, the Christian servant-leader receives a new definition. *The leader is one who, understanding his or her own spiritual gifts, builds a ministry of inreach and outreach on the basis of the identification of the spiritual gifts in others.*

The goal is always to strive for a complete ministry of inreach and outreach under grace. The local pastor of a small country church and the senior minister of a larger membership congregation are *both* servant-leaders. As such, they are stewards of the gifts of God in the Body of Christ.

Discovering the Servant-Leader's Gifts

Each clergyperson possesses distinctive and recognizable gifts for ministry. This is God's plan for the church. Paul speaks authoritatively on this matter when he writes, "The gifts and the calling of God are irrevocable" (Rom. 11:29). Knowing those gifts and utilizing them properly demonstrates our faithfulness to God.

The path toward discovery of the gifts of the leader is not dissimilar to the path for all Christians. Perception of gifts comes through self-awareness, feedback, and the counsel of others. Discernment also comes through personal areas of interest and accomplishment. Most of us discover our gifts throughout the years of ministry. Some gifts may change. New gifts may emerge over the years.

How can we know our gifts? How can we fulfill the ancient advice of Socrates, "Know thyself," in a Christian context? Are there avenues through which we can discover and bring those gifts to light?

Initial insight comes through recognizing areas of joy or frustration in ministry. Most clergy experience certain parts of ministry that have greater appeal than others.

Perhaps you enjoy home visitation. You carve out large segments of each week for such contacts. Perhaps you prefer time to work alone in your study. Perhaps you easily remember names and details in large group gatherings. Perhaps moving through a crowd easily is energizing for you.

Or perhaps you prefer a quieter one-on-one style. Often we can make some initial judgments about God-given gifts simply by what we truly enjoy doing.

Interviews held with inquiring candidates for ministry over the years have been startlingly similar. When asked, "Why do you believe you are called to ministry?" the answer is, "I like working with people." Or, "I want to help people." Only occasionally does a candidate or young ordinand have a clear picture of his or her gifts.

Perhaps this is one reason why growing numbers of men and women enter the ministry as a second career. As persons mature, they have greater clarity as to their true vocational call.

Once in a local church setting, the daily work of ministry brings refinement of initial perceptions. The practice of ministry also brings an opportunity for further clarification. An intentional, continuous clarification of gifts should be done from the outset of one's clergy journey.

One woman made a decision for ministry in her early thirties after several years in special care nursing. However, the practice of ministry did not illuminate the gifts she had hoped to bring to that call. Eventually, she found full-time service as a hospice worker. Ministry with the dying combined the best of both vocational calls in her life. Her labors now reflect the multiple gifts of God.

Which parts of your ministry bring special joy to you? Which parts drag you down most often? Where do you see a growing edge? Where do people respond to your ministry most positively?

You may discover that preaching and writing are sources of joy and motivation in your life. On the other hand, you may discover that your best days come when you have made personal contacts in homes or hospitals, and additional contacts by phone.

You may discover meaning and joy in church administration and stewardship development. On the other hand, you may find that administrative details are a negative drain. You prefer walking the main street of a community meeting store owners, bankers, and mechanics—providing a pastoral influence and presence that can never be matched by managerial and organizational paperwork.

Refinement of some of my own gifts came in a variety of ways. I received a preaching award during my senior year at seminary. Preaching became the central joy of my calling. I claimed the gift with gratitude to God. I learned to adapt styles of preaching to varied listeners.

My theological school training seemed to create some barriers for members of my first congregation. They occasionally asked me not to refer to books and authors by name in my preaching. Apparently, some of them found such references intimidating in light of their own limited educational background. I obliged their preferences.

Fifteen years later, visiting teams from the pastor-parish committee of my present church came to hear me preach. Some of them commented that my pulpit style was too folksy, and *not* intellectually challenging. As I resumed occasional book and author references in the ensuing years, many members eagerly responded to such references as guidelines for their own reading! God gave me a preaching style which "fit" the needs of a specific constituency. The spiritual gift could adjust to a different setting.

Some ministers are best suited to suburban communities where expectations and educational levels are usually high. Others adapt best in small towns where churches operate differently—more of an easy, warm pastoral style in both congregation and community. Some clergy have gifts for city ministries. Others do best in rural settings. God knows and calls forth the gifts. One second career minister insisted that he be allowed to enroll in seminary courses that befit a ministry in the inner city. He was sure that God was calling him to the city. The seminary professors saw different gifts. They urged him to take courses appropriate to rural pastorates "just in case." A few years ago (after 35 years in ministry), this man was nominated by his peers as *"rural* pastor of the year"!

You may find that creative juices flow when you are preparing sermons of a pastoral nature. Attempts to be prophetic do not come as easily. In those moments, remember Paul's words, "Some are apostles, some prophets." Apostolic proclamation suits your call more than prophetic interpretation.

You may find an unusual combination of gifts in your life—gifts that do not seem "logical" in human terms. One clergy colleague has a pastoral heart and a highly effective hospital, shut-in, and bereavement ministry. At the same time, he is innately at home with computer technology and software. He combined those seeming opposites in effective ministry. The foolishness of God is wiser than human knowledge. God gives as God chooses.

Avenues to Self-Discovery in Leadership

Servant leaders who truly want to recognize their own gifts need periods of reflection. We need to go apart for a few hours or even a few days. Using the model of Jesus in the Gospel narratives (see, for example, Mark 1:12, 35), we look at our ministry. We ask questions. We may write in a personal diary for later review.

Occasional "sanctuary" time allows us to evaluate what is happening in our lives. We ask deeper questions and seek more thoughtful answers. We look at our personal ministry and the total ministry of the church with new eyes. No known substitute exists for such retreat experiences in the life of a servant of God.

Beyond the personal retreat experience, however, there are other tools for leadership gift discovery. The most effective means for initiating an inventory of leadership gifts is the input of others. Persons who have worked as staff colleagues or on a volunteer lay leadership team are the best source of such input. These persons have a vested interest in strengthening the gifts of the servant-leader. They find their areas of contribution enhanced as they "build up the body and strengthen the work of ministry."

Organize a one- or two-day group event. Participants are drawn from the leadership team of the church—whether elected officers, appointed volunteers, or staff. The theme of the time together is spiritual gifts. Bible study includes Ephesians 4 or one of the various New Testament passages on spiritual gifts.

In the opening hours of the event, each participant receives a supply of preprinted cards—one for each member of the group. The card looks something like this:

NAME _____

Three present or emerging spiritual gifts I see in you right now:

_____

_____

_____

An * indicates this is the gift I would most like to see you grow or train or develop in the coming year, or to allow God to grow in you.

Initials_____

In a closing time of worship, thanksgiving, and sharing, each retreat participant names and explains *one* of the gifts he or she has written about another member. Duplicate "naming" of gifts is inevitable. However, such duplication will reinforce the presence of one particular spiritual gift in an individual. After each person reads from his or her card on behalf of another, the card is given to that member as a keepsake. I have found that this experience brings new light and joy to the understanding of spiritual gifts. Always, this offering of gifts is an exceptional experience of Christian affirmation.

I know of no more helpful approach to the discovery of one's leadership gifts than this exercise. I retain my own small "package" of these cards from such a retreat a few years ago. I retrieve them periodically for review and reflection. While this exercise assists all participants in the leadership of the church, the clergy leader receives enormous personal benefit and insight for the ensuing leadership journey.

Self-awareness comes through several other channels as well. Books of biography and autobiography are of benefit. Read books that tell the story of a Christian leader's life and call. Learn how each one discovered gifts which led to some special emphasis in ministry. Examine how each one honed and exercised those gifts. A group of clergy leaders might consider a book discussion group that studies several books each year with the specific purpose of discernment for professional growth.

Seek continuing education events that seem to nurture emerging gifts. Workshops and lectures on preaching, pastoral care, administration, stewardship cultivation, and spiritual formation abound. One cannot possibly study in all areas. However, as some sense of a "growing edge" in ministry becomes apparent, select events which feed that growing edge. Become more selective as greater clarity develops. Tend to your gifts and train them.

Specific devotional time for the purpose of discerning one's own gifts is important. Read Ephesians, with a journal close at hand. Read the Pastoral Epistles in a similar fashion. Read with the constant prayer that God will give you awareness of your gifts for ministry and confidence in the use of those gifts.

Further practical insight comes through such tools as the Myers-Briggs Type Indicator (MBTI) or the Taylor-Johnson Temperament Analysis (TJTA).[2] While not specifically addressing spiritual issues, either of these tools adds self-awareness and will be confirmation of other indicators along the way.

The MBTI is especially beneficial for self-awareness as to how one relates to others. In the previous chapter, we saw the MBTI as a good tool for persons working on the same team. But the MBTI also provides insight toward understanding why certain areas of ministry are more appealing than others.

I discovered that the reason for my discomfort and rapid energy drain in large group social gatherings is due to inherent introversion. When a person is moderately introverted, meeting and making conversation with people is exhausting. On the other hand, when one is an extrovert, meeting and making conversation is energizing. This is why some are more comfortable working quietly in their study while others enjoy visitation or walking the streets of a small town community.

Myers-Briggs also helps us to understand why group decision making can bring conflict. If you are a person who prefers bringing issues to quick and definitive closure, you may find yourself in conflict with others. Other team members prefer to process decisions for a long time. They need to ask "one more question" or look at the situation from "one more perspective."

An effective Christian leader needs to know himself or herself. Then, understand what is happening in the group in order to allow individual personalities to work together more effectively. Utilization of this knowledge protects the group both from unnecessary conflict and patronizing leadership styles. When the leader is "first among equals," it is important to allow everyone to process in their own way. But, as leader, one must also know how to set boundaries of time and format so that one style does not dominate.

The other inventory, the Taylor-Johnson Temperament Analysis, identifies nine personality traits in a different fashion. TJTA places you in a profile with thousands of others who have taken the test. Are you tense or relaxed, depressed or lighthearted, subjective or objective, highly disciplined or mostly spontaneous? TJTA can also help you see yourself as others see you—depending upon how many persons are willing to answer the questions on your behalf.

While all of the above strategies can be helpful and are recommended, some are more beneficial than others. Were I to rank them, I would choose two as primary tools: (1) personal retreat and devotional time, accompanied by some journaling, and (2) the staff or leadership retreat exercise.

Some level of self-discovery is essential. Knowing your own strengths and gifts is a mandate for effective leadership in the church. Whatever tools you select, do so in a true ecclesiology of spiritual gifts.

Once Your Gifts Are Identified

Now you are ready for the next steps. However, a word of caution: make certain God's leadership is operative, not what you *wish* your gifts could be. It is easy to understand that one does not have vocal music *abilities*! But it is not as easy to discern whether a *spiritual gift* is of God or one of mere human desire.

You may wish to touch the lives of youth, but find language styles difficult. Or you have unrealistic expectations regarding their conduct. You may wish to hold a prestigious pulpit, but be more suited to small church ministry. You may yearn for the skills in offering profound public prayers, but be far more effective in bedside prayers in the hospital room. *Know* your true gifts—by the grace of God and the work of the Holy Spirit. Accurate discernment is exceedingly important.

There once was an older couple who lived a somewhat reclusive existence for many years. One day, the husband went into town. He returned with an old cello that had only one string. He began playing the same note, continuing for hours every day.

Finally, his wife also went to town. She returned to inform him of her discovery: "Husband, cellos have four strings, not two. What's more, the hand of the player moves up and down those strings, making many notes of beautiful music. Why do you insist on playing the same note day after day?"

"Listen, wife," replied the man. "All those people out there are still trying to find their note. I, at least, have found mine!"

Once you know your gifts, begin to form the primary emphases of your ministry around those gifts. If you are prompted by God to work hard on the proclamation of the word, stay with it! If you are compelled by the Spirit to be with people as many hours of the working day as possible, do it!

Two large churches were established at the same time in a community. One grew on the strength of a senior minister who was a gifted orator, but who had limited pastoral skills with members and staff. The other church grew on the strength of a pastor who moved among people easily, related to them in effective pastoral ways, but whose abilities in the pulpit were less than exciting. Both churches thrived because *each leader knew their own gifts well.* Meanwhile, their respective staffs supplied other vital gifts necessary to complete the ministry of Jesus Christ.

If you are a good pastoral preacher, use your pulpit to express the healing care and love of God for people in all life situations. If, on the other hand, you are very intentional in providing individual pastoral care, your pulpit may be used for teaching or prophetic ministries with greater frequency. If your people sense God's presence through your personal, caring contact, they will overlook less than profound preaching.

If you are called to teach, make your teaching worthy of God's gifts at work in you. A solid biblical teaching ministry strengthens the church.

The gift of dreaming or visioning is a special spiritual gift. One minister was superbly gifted as a visionary. He could plant the dreams but needed assistance in turning dreams into action. He gathered a group together for breakfast one Saturday morning each month at a local restaurant. He would spend thirty to forty minutes with them espousing the latest dreams he held in his heart. The group would listen in fascination, and resonate in some awe at the quality and power of his vision. He would then leave them alone to wrestle with the mechanics of the matters at hand. He did not shy away completely from the nitty gritty of details in his ministry. He simply knew the parameters of his best gifts.

Use your gifts well. Find others who can do those things for which you are not suited. Synergy comes from the combined spiritual gifts of many to form a wonderful wholeness. Such is the plan of God for the church.

As you begin to find validation in the exercise of your gifts, enter into further dialogue with those who are most closely related to you in the congregation. Advise them of the discoveries you are making. Ask for candid feedback. Invite them to suggest ways in which the whole ministry of the church may be enhanced by the direction in which you sense God is leading.

Share your awareness of any emerging gifts with the appropriate personnel committee of the church. Tell them where you believe God is leading you. Do not hesitate to suggest specific goals. "During the next two years, I will be focusing upon _____ in my ministry with this church. Here is where I believe I am stronger by God's grace. I ask for your wisdom and feedback as I concentrate in this area of study and self-development." Frequently, you will find clarity for your ministry by regularly making such statements out loud. Hearing oneself articulate the possibility of gifts can bring confirmation as to the direction of your growth. And remember: never neglect the opportunity to encourage exploration of spiritual gifts in the lives of those on the committee!

Senior clergy and leaders of staff should not become restricted specialists. Servant leaders do not luxuriate in some exclusive niche of ministry. Exercising your particular gifts is a valid expression of concentration; but not to the detriment of other areas. In most churches, neither paperwork or pastoral contact can be ignored. Many daily office tasks and faithful pastoral duties complement other gifts.

Seeds of Encouragement

Paul writes, "Now we have received not the spirit of the world, but the Spirit that is from God, *so that we may understand the gifts bestowed on us by God*" (1 Cor. 2:12; *emphasis mine*). The model for leadership which is proposed in these pages is not one that can be set in motion without regular attention and monitoring. Read for insight and augmentation. Maintain regular contact with coworkers and colleagues.

The model also requires constant reinforcement through prayer and a devotional lifestyle. The work of the Holy Spirit is best discerned through a disciplined prayer life—one which includes a great deal of listening. The only way to avoid pitfalls and ego traps is with regular prayer before the Author of all gifts.

A congregation built upon the theology of spiritual gifts must always believe in moving on *toward* perfection. There will be problems. The system is not perfect precisely because we are human vessels. Frequently, the ego will get in the way. Someone has suggested that "Ego" stands for "Edge God out." We can easily edge God out and move ahead with our own agendas.

Someone asked Mark Twain about the reason for his success. He replied, "I was born excited."

I empathize with that remark. God continually provides me with a fresh dose of excitement regarding a ministry grounded in spiritual gifts.

Jesus' earthly ministry with his first disciples frequently necessitated a ministry of encouragement. I receive my own gift from the One who gave it so generously to his inner circle of followers. One illustrative passage on this theme is found in Mark: "He also said, 'The kingdom of God is as if someone would scatter seed on the ground, and would sleep and rise night and day, and the seed would sprout and grow, he does not know how' " (4:26-27).

The original setting for the telling of this parable is vivid in my mind. The disciples ponder the effectiveness of what they are doing. They know a growing discouragement and disappointment in their ranks. They ask one another, "Is all of this going to amount to anything? Will it make a difference that we were here? Will these throngs of people ever become what Jesus seems to want to help them become?"

Jesus, hearing their doubt and hesitancy, says simply, "Listen! Let me tell you a brief parable—about a seed that grows secretly." The parable gives specific encouragement to resident skeptics. "All you can do is plant the seed," he says. "Leave growing and bearing fruit to God." Jesus probably used this parable on more than one occasion.

The writer of Ephesians offers an heartening word as he drafts a general letter to the churches. "In Christ we have also obtained an inheritance, having been destined according to the purpose of him who accomplishes all things according to his counsel and will, so that we, who were the first to set our hope on Christ, might live for the praise of his glory" (Eph. 1:11-12).

When this same writer moves to the theme of spiritual gifts in 4:11-12, he is still offering encouragement. "This is how the church is meant to be," he proclaims. "You are given gifts from the very heart of God."

The words of Ephesians are a challenge to the church. We are instruments of hope among the people of God. Paul reminds us that the Scriptures were written "So that by steadfastness and by the encouragement of the scriptures we might have hope" (Rom. 15:4).

The New Testament witness calls each of us to steady reassurance. The church is a channel for inspiration to people at all stages of growing faith. Amid a plethora of important roles to fulfill, the church is fundamentally called today to train, encourage, and dispatch disciples. We return to the "gathering place" regularly to be rejuvenated and recharged.

On the day I arrived to begin my new ministry in the South Hills of Pittsburgh, I found a potted plant in my office. The plant was a gift from a Christian friend in my former congregation. Amidst the foliage, she had strategically placed a small lapel button from a congregational financial campaign. The button read simply, "Make it happen!" The plant still flourishes in my office fifteen years later. New roots and new foliage have come and gone. The plant provides a small symbol for what I believe most about the ministry. Under the power of grace, we must encourage the people of God. By the gifts of the Spirit working in us, we make it happen!

We do not make things happen by ourselves. We are instruments of God's Spirit. According to the grace given to us, we can join hands, lean into the winds of the Spirit, and bring new possibilities to the local congregation. Putting our hands into God's hand, we can make it happen. A theology of spiritual gifts is a God-given means to that end.

APPENDIX

These position descriptions provide representative samples of the work discussed in chapter 5. Each of them has been modified and abbreviated slightly to be more helpful to the reader. They are intended as models from which to work in the development of such documents in a church of any size.

A. Senior Minister of Preaching

The following represents the major portion of the author's current position description. The document suggests present discernment of spiritual gifts for church oversight as well as leadership for a "teaching church."

1. Primary responsibility for pulpit ministry with a minimum of thirty-eight preaching weekends plus Christmas Eve each year. Recognized use of major blocks of time for preparation of this pulpit ministry, including occasional personal retreats. Assignment of associate clergy and guests to the pulpit.
2. Approximately three days each month (and occasional extended periods) for writing, teaching, preaching, or lecturing for the larger church.
3. Oversee the ministry and mission of the church, utilizing the gifts of staff.

4. General oversight of designated staff through (a) consultative development and maintaining position descriptions, (b) annual reviews with clergy and program staff in relation to their position descriptions, (c) recommending changes, reallocation, dismissals, or additions to staff through SPRC, (d) annual development of salary recommendations for all staff through SPRC, (e) advising and approving plans for staff continuing education, and (f) providing resources and support for staff care and morale. Assign similar oversight of some support staff to others.

5. Principal responsibility for financial and stewardship development throughout the congregation.

6. Write approximately thirty columns each year for the weekly church newsletter.

7. Maintain personal contact with representative members and groups including (a) Monday evening phone calls to all first time worship visitors, (b) consultation and counseling with members as requested and available, (c) a proportionate share of weddings, baptisms, and funerals/memorial services, (d) teaching one adult Sunday school class and two short-term adult classes each year, and (e) at least two afternoons each month for hospital visitation.

B. *Minister for Congregational Care*

The following is an example of a clergy associate description which targets one major area of the church's life. The position assumes some secretarial support and assistance.

1. Primary responsibility for the work of congregational care, including: (a) administration of a congregational neighborhood plan, (b) oversight of updating and maintaining membership records, (c) care for the tape ministry to shut-ins, hospitality groups, parking lot attendants, and the prayer chain. Assist in recruiting and training persons with gifts of leadership in each of these areas.

2. Primary responsibility for a church-wide program of lay pastoral care including design, training, assignment, continuing education, and periodic evaluation.

3. Primary responsibility for the shut-in ministry of the church—coordinated with other clergy staff and the lay pastors.

4. Primary responsibility for coordinating specific pastoral services of the church, including weddings, baptisms, and funerals. Assign these services through the year in consultation with the other clergy.
5. Provide or assign lay or clergy follow-up visitation in instances of recent hospitalization or bereavement. The follow-up shall be monitored until sufficient healing takes place and/or assigned lay pastoral care is in place.
6. Coordinate pastoral visits to hospitals with other clergy.
7. Worship, liturgy, and preaching assignments as assigned in consultation with the senior minister.

C. Minister for the Seeker Initiative and Singles

The following was a newly developed position description in 1995, incorporating a successful and active singles ministry with a new worship and evangelism initiative for seekers.

1. Develop and implement an alternative worship opportunity based on a "seeker sensitive" model using a carefully selected planning team of laity and staff. Assume primary preaching responsibility for this service each week. Development presupposes some acquaintance with contemporary Christian music as an important component of the alternative worship service.
2. Responsibility for oversight and expansion of a multifaceted singles ministry including program development, staff liaison to a singles council, and leadership development among single adults. Direct leadership responsibilities for the divorce recovery ministry. Assignment of lay pastors in the singles ministry in consultation with the minister for congregational care.
3. Pastoral visits to hospitals as coordinated with minister for congregational care each week.
4. Worship liturgist and occasional preaching responsibilities in the more traditional settings as assigned in consultation with the senior minister.
5. Work closely with the clergy and lay program staff in regular planning, implementation, and review of program, spiritual life, and ministry of the church. Settings for this include weekly staff meetings, informal gatherings, one-on-one consultation time with the senior minister, and staff retreats.

D. Director of Choirs

The following represents a "matured" position description after remarkable growth from limited part-time choir leadership to major responsibility for the total choral program. The person currently in this position is diaconal (a consecrated lay order in The United Methodist Church).

1. Direct responsibility for adult and youth choirs, two children's choirs, and bell choir. Recruit volunteer directors and accompanists for other children's choirs as appropriate.
2. Select and calendar all choral music.
3. Oversee and supervise the work of part-time music staff for all choral, handbell, and liturgical dance choirs.
4. Arrange summer soloists and special music schedule.
5. Pastoral care of choir families, communicating needs to clergy staff. Cultivate a strong caring ministry of choir families to one another.
6. Oversee choir parent programs for children and youth.
7. Arrange occasional music reading and voice classes for youth and adults.
8. Assume responsibility for a plan of choir recruitment. Develop potential choir singers. Work toward maximum participation in choir membership.
9. Direct oversight of the music committee, including the recruitment and training of lay leadership for that committee coordinated with the work of the nominating committee.
10. Develop and monitor an annual music budget.
11. Oversee volunteers for updating and maintenance of the choir library.

E. Organist and Director of Worship Life

The following represents the combination of organ keyboard skills with worship administration skills to constitute one full-time position.

1. Plan and develop liturgical resources for all regular and special worship services in consultation with the senior minister.
2. Arrange for the production of all worship materials, bulletins, special programs—working to ensure that all of these materials are useful tools of clear communication.

3. Responsibility for the work of the worship committee, altar guild, and ushers. Responsibility shall include recruiting and training of persons with gifts of lay leadership in these areas.
4. Recommend and monitor worship budgets for each year.
5. Provide organ leadership for all regular and special worship services. Be available for church weddings and funeral (memorial) services as requested. (It is understood that a significant portion of time each week will be devoted to practice at the organ console.)
6. Coordinate mechanical aspects of Sunday morning and seasonal worship services: lighting, communion, special sanctuary setups, devices for the hearing impaired, baptism, acolytes, furnishings, and the sound system.
7. Oversee volunteers for the sanctuary sound system and other worship-related audio equipment.
8. Supervise the care and maintenance of all church-owned musical instruments, robes, vestments, and worship supplies.
9. Regularly assess and advise the church with regard to worship accessibility to persons with handicapping conditions.

F. Diaconal Minister with Youth

The following represents a position description which explores a diverse array of possibilities in a person who has the capacity for such diversity. This is the second of two positions which are currently diaconal (consecrated lay persons in The United Methodist Church).

1. Develop all ministry with junior and senior high youth, including Sunday school, youth fellowship groups, work camps, service projects, and other possibilities that encompass both the inreach and outreach of the church.
2. Recruit, train, and utilize all youth church school leaders and youth fellowship advisors.
3. Develop a strong youth coordinating council. Select persons with lay leadership in these areas coordinated with the committee on nominations.
4. Design and implement confirmation training of eighth grade youth and families. Utilize the input and direct involvement of clergy staff as appropriate. Review the need for confirmation training of older youth.

5. Give special attention to the spiritual growth ministry with youth. Develop "branch groups" each school year within covenant discipleship models.

6. Visit the homes of youth and their families and/or provide arenas for listening to input from youth and youth families regarding needs and hopes. Such contact will also sustain essential qualities of lay pastoral care.

7. Provide oversight and leadership to ministries related to college age youth and other post-high school young adults.

G. Director of Christian Formation and Program

The following represents the end result of growth in one individual on staff to a position of remarkable authority and skill. Note that a lay person in this position does not oversee clergy staff except regarding programmatic issues.

1. Oversee the total program design of the church to ensure depth, quality, and faithfulness. Particular attention shall be placed upon a healthy and vital balance between inreach and outreach. Develop models for Christian formation in personal discipleship and in congregational life.

2. Dialogue regularly with program staff, clergy staff in program areas, and directors of church-related outreach components. Such dialogue shall include insight and oversight regarding current programs in process, new ministries in various stages of design, and careful coordination to avoid unnecessary schedule or administrative conflict.

3. Oversee the program planning body of the church including (a) coordinating the overall program, (b) retreats and planning days, (c) recommending annual ministry goals, and (d) establishing healthy, realistic budgets.

4. Design and implement leadership development for all elected and appointed program persons.

5. Give specific time and attention to the adult, family, and outreach ministries.

6. Shared responsibility with the senior minister for ongoing nurture of covenant discipleship groups and discipleship guides.

7. Maintain appropriate information so as to help select persons with the most obvious spiritual gifts for elected lay leadership throughout the church. Attend meetings of the nominating committee in the absence of the senior minister.

8. Represent the senior minister at committees and short-term task forces at his request.

9. Regularly consult with the senior minister regarding issues which need input and which affect the life of the church, especially discipleship, Christian formation, staff morale, and administrative policy.

10. Preside at weekly staff meetings in the absence of the senior minister.

H. *Director of Church Growth and Communications*

The following description represents a unique package of gifts in one individual, probably atypical in most personnel situations. The description requires both extrovert and introvert energy.

1. Responsibility for the new member program. Communication and listening to new residents and nonaffiliated persons in the community. Work with the evangelism committee to assist in this process.

2. Full responsibility for a multifaceted follow-up procedure for all first time visitors using personal contact, correspondence, printed resources, and staff assistance.

3. Plan and carry out the program of welcoming those persons who make a decision to join the church, including orientation and membership reception. Continuously evaluate the process with the senior minister and staff.

4. Primary responsibility for active assimilation of persons into the life of the church once they have joined, and for ascertaining the depth of involvement for about one year after they join.

5. Advise the nominating committee as to the best utilization of the gifts of newest members.

6. Provide initial guidance and oversight to all small groups which arise out of the evangelism efforts. Work to develop indigenous leadership in such groups after a time so that energy may be focused on newer groups.

7. Primary responsibility for the weekly church newsletter: collecting materials for copy, writing, layout, editing, and photography.

8. Maintain close contact with publicity arms beyond the local church for maximum exposure: local news media, local editions of newspapers, and district and/or conference newsletter editions.
9. Work closely with the annual financial campaign efforts to develop the strongest possible publicity.

I. Director of Stewardship and Computer Services

The following is a relatively new position which has emerged over the years, and which now incorporates major responsibility in the staff configuration.

1. Maintain and supervise all records of financial giving, keeping contributing households informed on a regular basis.
2. Provide financial data on stewardship to the finance committee, and assist in interpretation of such data.
3. Coordinate all financial campaigns. Research and recommend appropriate strategies, resources, leadership persons, and calendaring for such campaigns. Work closely with the chair of each regular and special campaign committee to ensure the best possible flow of program as well as communication with the congregation.
4. Serve as the primary computer systems manager, working to ensure the best possible utilization of all computers in all offices. Make recommendations on repair and replacement. Supervise and control those responsible for making entries, changes, and corrections in any computer data.
5. Assist the staff in valuing and appreciating all persons who serve as volunteers in any aspect of the above.

J. Senior Administrative Assistant and Music Associate

The following position represents a new development which moves one person beyond routine administrative duties to an additional recognition of gifts in music program.

1. Primary responsibility for secretarial support for the senior minister and two other program staff. Allocate some work through volunteers when appropriate.
2. Administrative support for the senior minister shall include placing phone calls, making appointments, handling correspondence, pro-

tecting private office times, preparing sermon manuscripts for print-ing and mailing, and scheduling meetings and consultations.
3. Responsibility for developing and maintaining the calendar of space usage throughout the church. Negotiate changes with church and nonchurch groups which use the building.
4. Serve as director of one children's choir, using one weekday afternoon for preparation time.
5. Accompany the youth choir on annual choir tour and at all rehearsals in preparation for the tour.
6. Fulfill necessary responsibilities as official corporate secretary of the church. Provide notary public duties for the church as needed.

K. Building Maintenance Supervisor

This position description provides parameters for one person to have total oversight of all property and mechanical systems.

1. Oversight of all matters pertaining to building and grounds, including church owned pastoral residences. This shall include contact with various contract services for mechanical services, mechanical sys-tems, landscaping, pest control, snow removal, and others as author-ized by the trustees.
2. Oversight of all full-time and part-time custodial staff, including interviewing, hiring, conveying salary, benefits, and other work con-cerns.
3. Regular dialogue with the staff with regard to maintaining good communication and morale of custodial staff, and the most effective use of time and space to optimize ministry and mission.
4. Report regularly to the monthly meeting of the trustees.
5. Oversee volunteer work groups at the church on a regular or occa-sional basis.
6. Oversee or delegate care and upkeep of the church van(s).
7. Arrange for the best methods for emergency or urgent contact in unexpected developments as they may arise.

NOTES

1. Groundings

1. Even though the book begins with a greeting to "the saints who are in Ephesus" (Eph. 1:1), most scholars conclude that the total letter lacks the style of a letter to a specific church.
2. Much of this early personal history documents the years at St. Paul's United Methodist Church in the North Hills of Pittsburgh from 1971 to 1980. The congregation was a mission church started in 1967. Today, it has a membership of almost 1,500.
3. Neither of these numbers include administrative support and sexton staff. However, these persons are integral to the total leadership team. Today, most of them are also members of the congregation—consistent with my ecclesiology of spiritual gifts.

2. Directions

1. The master mind of the theology of spiritual gifts, Paul, had no prior indication of his call to apostleship.
2. See, for example, Romans 12:3-8, 1 Corinthians 12-14, 1 Peter 4:10-11, 1 Timothy 4:13, and, of course, Ephesians 4:11.
3. For example, the gift of developing print or video media that will appropriately communicate the gospel to a generation raised on sound bytes, "bullet" notices, and visual stimulation.
4. These two words reflect my own terminology used over many years. The reader will find reference to them in other parts of this book.
5. Christ Church offers communion at least three times each week—including early Sunday morning, the close of Saturday evening worship, and at midweek. The church has offered a week night service of communion, intercessory prayer, and healing for nearly forty years. This thirty minute service is a mainstay of each week's worship opportunities.
6. From a "Pastor's Desk" column by William M. Easum, at the time, senior minister of the Colonial Hills United Methodist Church of San Antonio, Texas. vol. XX, no. 31, August 2, 1992, 1, 3.

3. Claiming Traditional Gifts

1. See, for example, Acts 20:28. Quite possibly, bishops and overseers were the same designation. I find the term "overseer" to be the most usable biblical term for my theology of leadership.

2. The following example is adapted from one of the Serendipity Workshops led by Lyman Coleman.
3. My personal practice is to take several two- to three-day personal retreats each year as a normal part of my ministry. I use a variety of settings: a motel room, a retreat center, the vacation home of a church member. The purpose is truly to be removed from the everyday routine and distractions.
4. An example of such printed tools is: *Gifts Discovery Workshop* by Herbert Mather (Nashville: Discipleship Resources, 1985). The tool utilizes both a member's workbook and a study guide.
5. At the time of my first introduction to the lay pastor ministry in 1978, Dr. Sunderland was on the staff of the Institute of Religion in Houston, Texas. To the best of my knowledge, no textbook or training manual was ever written on the subject. He used lectures and verbatims of actual lay pastoral visitations in his training model.
6. This is the primary teaching tool utilized by Sunderland in his training several years ago. I still regard it as a useful vehicle, both in initial training and in continuing education sessions. Supervising clergy may decide to create a verbatim from the visit by a member of the training group—maintaining all issues of confidentiality.
7. In some congregations, consecrated elements are placed in the hands of lay pastors during the liturgy for communion. Lay pastors are then sent from the service of worship directly to the homes of those who are to receive. In congregations with multiple services, an excellent opportunity for this process exists at the first service of the morning. Shut-ins and others receive the sacrament at approximately the same time as their church family is receiving it at the building during the second hour of worship.
8. Some examples: "Does this mean we won't see the minister anymore?" or "What will the *real* pastor do with his or her time now?" or "Isn't that what we pay our minister to do?" or "I only want Rev. Smith coming to see me, and nobody else!"
9. Perhaps the best tool for this kind of annual or semiannual study is Maxie Dunnam, *The Workbook of Intercessory Prayer* (Nashville: The Upper Room, 1979).

4. Discovering Emerging Gifts

1. See my book *Right on the Money* (Nashville: Discipleship Resources, 1994). The book contains four sections of sermons on financial stewardship, with an emphasis upon discipleship growing through generous giving.
2. Such referral almost always brings less than adventurous results. Financial advisors are generally very conservative on behalf of their clients. Unless they are courageous givers in their own lives, they are not likely to understand the gift of giving in the lives of their clients.
3. As told by Norman Neaves, senior minister of The Church of the Servant in Oklahoma City, OK.
4. Actually, I prefer "household" to "family" in church communication. "Household" is a good biblical word, and never excludes any person in its scope.
5. The best introduction to this particular small group ministry is found in David Lowes Watson, *Covenant Discipleship: Christian Formation Through Mutual Accountability* (Nashville: Discipleship Resources, 1991).
6. The brief outline of what follows is gleaned from lectures and conversations with David Watson.

5. Staffing: Building a Team

1. This principle does not normally include clergy. The special gifts of clergy will be discussed later in the chapter.
2. I recently raised sufficient seed money to initiate a part-time food service ministry in our congregation. Similar gifts were sought and given when we hired a full-time organist and director of worship life and a full-time director of youth ministries.
3. This project was mentioned earlier in chapter 2.
4. A sample of the most current position descriptions for several representative members of my church staff team is attached in the appendix.

LINCOLN CHRISTIAN COLLEGE AND SEMINARY

5. In United Methodist polity, this is the staff-parish relations committee, comprised of ten persons. Some congregations have two separate committees—one for clergy staff and one for lay staff. I prefer one committee carefully deployed, and one which holds me accountable for appropriate staff oversight. The arrangement also seems appropriate for the ministry of spiritual gifts.
6. I have occasionally discovered that tensions between myself and another staff member are far more disruptive to the other staff than they are to me. What may be an insult or frustration to the leader may be almost immobilizing to other members of the staff.
7. See chapter 6 for more details on this.
8. A position description for a minister for congregational care is included in the appendix.
9. A second associate clergy position in the appendix suggests a *combined* ministry with the "seeker initiative" and with single adults.
10. The center serves approximately 350 children each week in five separate components, and employs 60 persons in full- or part-time leadership.
11. For a helpful basic discussion of the MBTI, see David Keirsey and Marilyn Bates, *Please Understand Me: Character and Temperament Types* (Del Mar, Calif.: Prometheus Nemesis Book Company, 1984). A number of church leaders are certified to conduct the testing process and assist a staff in analyzing the results.
12. David Albert Farmer, "Church Staff Relationships: An Interview with Roy Oswald," *Pulpit Digest*, March/April 1993, 74.

6. Knowing Self: Gifts of the Leader

1. See his *Servant Leadership: A Journey into the Nature of Legitimate Power and Greatness* (New York: Paulist Press, 1977), 241. See also p. 19 in Greenleaf's introduction.
2. The Myers-Briggs resource is noted in chapter 4. The Taylor-Johnson Temperament Analysis is distributed by Psychological Publications, Inc. 5300 Hollywood Blvd., Los Angeles, CA 90027. Sample materials and a catalog are available. The TJTA's best value comes when completed by yourself *and at least one other person* who knows you well—a spouse, close friend, or someone with whom you have daily contact.